D0462838

Townsend, John Rowe, comp.
    Modern poetry: a selection. Photographs by Barbara
Pfeffer. ₁1st American ed.₎ Philadelphia. Lippincott
₍1974₎

    224 p. illus. 24 cm.

    SUMMARY: More than 135 poems by modern English and Amer-
ican poets including W. H. Auden, Dylan Thomas, Sylvia Plath, and
Randall Jarrell.

    1. English poetry—20th century.   2. American poetry—20th cen-
tury. ₁1. English poetry—20th century. 2. American poetry—20th
century₎   I. Pfeffer, Barbara, illus. II. Title.

PR1225.T64   1974   821'.9'108   73-7736
ISBN 0-397-31477-9   MARC

                                    74 ₁4₎   ▲0

MODERN POETRY

A SELECTION BY
JOHN ROWE TOWNSEND

PHOTOGRAPHS BY BARBARA PFEFFER

J. B. LIPPINCOTT COMPANY
PHILADELPHIA AND NEW YORK

U.S. Library of Congress Cataloging in Publication Data

Townsend, John Rowe, comp.
  Modern poetry.

  SUMMARY: More than 135 poems by modern English and American poets
including W. H. Auden, Dylan Thomas, Sylvia Plath, and Randall Jarrell.
    1. English poetry—20th century. 2. American poetry—20th century. [1. English
poetry—20th century. 2. American poetry—20th century] I. Pfeffer, Barbara, illus.
II. Title.
PR1225.T64   1974   821'.9'108   73-7736
ISBN-0-397-31477-9

SOURCES AND ACKNOWLEDGMENTS

W. H. AUDEN, b. 1907. "Musée des Beaux Arts" copyright 1940 and renewed 1968 by
  W. H. Auden. Reprinted from *Collected Shorter Poems 1927–1957,* by permission of
  Random House, Inc. "On This Island" and "O what is that sound" copyright 1937
  and renewed 1965 by W. H. Auden. Reprinted from *Collected Shorter Poems 1927–
  1957,* by permission of Random House, Inc.
GEORGE BARKER, b. 1913. "On a Friend's Escape from Drowning off the Norfolk
  Coast" from *Collected Poems 1930 to 1965.* Copyright © 1957, 1962, and 1965 by
  George Granville Barker. Reprinted by permission of October House, Inc.
PATRICIA BEER, b. 1924. "A Dream of Hanging" from *Just Like the Resurrection*
  (Macmillan & Co. Ltd., 1967). Reprinted with the permission of Macmillan, London
  and Basingstoke.
ANNE BERESFORD, b. 1929. "Saturday in New York" and "The Romanies in Town"
  from *The Lair* (Rapp & Whiting Ltd., 1968).
JOHN BETJEMAN, b. 1906. "Cornish Cliffs," "Dorset," and "The Licorice Fields at Ponte-
  fract" from *Collected Poems* (John Murray Ltd., 1970; Houghton Mifflin Co. Inc.).
  "Cornish Cliffs" originally in *High and Low* (1966). "Dorset" originally in *A Continual
  Dew* (1937).
D. M. BLACK, b. 1941. "The Educators" from *The Educators* (Barrie & Rockliff Ltd.,
  1969).
EDWARD BRATHWAITE, b. 1930. "Chad," "Mmenson," and "Timbuctu" from *Masks*
  (Oxford University Press, 1968).
EDWIN BROCK, b. 1927. "Evolution" from *A Cold Day at the Zoo* (Rapp & Whiting Ltd.,

1970). "Song of the Battery Hen" from *Penguin Modern Poets 8* (Penguin Books Ltd., 1966).

ALAN BROWNJOHN, b. 1931. "The Rabbit," the second of "Two poems after Prevert" from *The Railings* (Digby Press, 1961).

CHARLES CAUSLEY, b. 1917. "Ballad of the Bread Man" from *Underneath the Water* (Rupert Hart-Davis Ltd., 1968). "Innocent's Song" from *Johnny Alleluia* (Rupert Hart-Davis Ltd., 1961). "Timothy Winters" from *Union Street* (Rupert Hart-Davis Ltd., 1957).

TONY CONNOR, b. 1930. "Above Penmaenmawr" from *Kon in Springtime* (Oxford University Press, 1968). "Elegy for Alfred Hubbard" from *With Love Somehow* (Oxford University Press, 1962).

R. N. CURREY, b. 1907. "Unseen Fire," first two sections of "Disintegration of Springtime" from *This Other Planet* (Routledge & Kegan Paul Ltd., 1945).

ROBERT DUNCAN, b. 1919. "The Ballad of Mrs Noah" from *The Opening of the Field* (Evergreen Books Ltd., 1960).

D. J. ENRIGHT, b. 1920. "Dreaming in the Shanghai Restaurant" from *Addictions* (Chatto & Windus Ltd., 1962). "The Quagga" from *Some Men Are Brothers* (Chatto & Windus Ltd., 1960).

DAVID GASCOYNE, b. 1916. "Snow in Europe" from *Collected Poems* (Oxford University Press, 1965); originally in *Poems 1937–1942* (Poetry, London, 1943).

ZULFIKAR GHOSE, b. 1935. "Geography Lesson" from *Jets from Orange* (Macmillan & Co. Ltd., 1967). Reprinted with the permission of Macmillan, London and Basingstoke. "This Landscape, These People" from *The Loss of India* (Routledge & Kegan Paul Ltd., 1964).

THOM GUNN, b. 1929. "Incident on a Journey" reprinted by permission of Faber & Faber Ltd. from *Fighting Terms* (1962); originally published by Fantasy Press (1954). "Jesus and His Mother" reprinted by permission of Faber & Faber Ltd. from *The Sense of Movement* (1957). "Touch" reprinted by permission of Faber & Faber Ltd. from *Touch* (1967).

DONALD HALL, b. 1928. From *The Alligator Bride:* "By the Exeter River," copyright © 1969 by Donald Hall; "In the Kitchen of the Old House," copyright © 1969 by Donald Hall; "The Old Pilot" (originally titled "The Old Pilot's Death") copyright © 1963 by Donald Hall. Reprinted by permission of Harper & Row Publishers, Inc.

SEAMUS HEANEY, b. 1939. "Digging" from *Death of a Naturalist,* copyright © 1966 by Seamus Heaney. Reprinted by permission of Oxford University Press, Inc.

JOHN HEATH-STUBBS, b. 1918. "Epitaph" from *Selected Poems* (Oxford University Press, 1965). "The Starling" from *The Blue-Fly in the Head* (Oxford University Press, 1962).

ADRIAN HENRI, b. 1932. "Adrian Henri's Talking After Christmas Blues" and "Tonight at Noon" from *Tonight at Noon,* published by David McKay Co., Inc. Copyright © 1969 by Adrian Henri. Reprinted by permission of the publisher.

PHILIP HOBSBAUM, b. 1932. "The Place's Fault" from *The Place's Fault and Other Poems* (Macmillan & Co. Ltd., 1964). Reprinted with permission of Macmillan, London and Basingstoke.

TED HUGHES, b. 1930. "Hawk Roosting" and "Pike" from *Lupercal,* copyright © 1959 by Ted Hughes. "Thistles" from *Wodwo,* copyright © 1961 by Ted Hughes. "Wind" from *The Hawk in the Rain,* copyright © 1956 by Ted Hughes. Reprinted by permission of Harper & Row, Publishers, Inc.

RANDALL JARRELL, 1914–1965. "Bats" reprinted with permission of The Macmillan Company from *The Bat-Poet.* Copyright © 1963, 1964 by The Macmillan Company. "The Lonely Man" from *The Woman at the Washington Zoo.* Copyright © 1954 by Randall Jarrell. Reprinted by permission of Atheneum Publishers, Inc. Appeared originally in *Poetry.* Both poems appear in *Complete Poems* (Farrar, Straus & Giroux, Inc., 1968).

ELIZABETH JENNINGS, b. 1926. "My Grandmother" and "One Flesh" from *Collected Poems* (Macmillan & Co. Ltd., 1967). Reprinted with the permission of Macmillan, London and Basingstoke. "My Grandmother" originally in *Song for a Birth or a Death* (1961). "One Flesh" originally in *The Mind Has Mountains* (1966).

EVAN JONES, b. 1927. "Lament of the Banana Man" and "Song of the Banana Man" from *Caribbean Voices* (Evans Brothers Ltd., 1966). "Song of the Banana Man" published by "Bim," Bridgetown, Barbados (1952).

JENNY JOSEPH, b. 1932. "Warning" from *New Poems 1965*, the twelfth P.E.N. Anthology of Contemporary Poetry (Hutchinson Publishing Group Ltd., 1966).

ROSEMARY JOSEPH, b. 1927. "Baking Day" from *A Group Anthology* (Oxford University Press, 1963).

PATRICK KAVANAGH, b. 1905. "If ever you go to Dublin town" from *Collected Poems* (MacGibbon & Kee Ltd., 1964).

RICHARD KELL, b. 1927. "Fishing Harbour towards Evening" and "The Pay Is Good" from *Control Tower* (Chatto & Windus Ltd., 1962).

JAMES KIRKUP, b. 1918. "Love in a Space-Suit" from *The Descent into the Cave* (Oxford University Press, 1957). "Tea in a Space-Ship" from *The Prodigal Son* (Oxford University Press, 1959).

PHILIP LARKIN, b. 1922. "An Arundel Tomb" reprinted by permission of Faber & Faber Ltd. from *The Whitsun Weddings*.

LAURIE LEE, b. 1914. "April Rise" from *The Bloom of Candles* (John Lehmann, 1947). "Milkmaid" from *The Sun My Monument*. All rights reserved. Reprinted by permission of Wesleyan University Press.

ALUN LEWIS, 1915–1944. "Goodbye" from *Ha! Ha! Among the Trumpets* (George Allen & Unwin Ltd., 1945); also appeared in *Selected Poetry and Prose* (1966).

C. DAY LEWIS, b. 1904. "Circus Lion" © 1962, "Watching Post" © 1954 by C. Day Lewis. Reprinted by permission of Harold Matson Company, Inc.

DOUGLAS LIVINGSTONE, b. 1932. "Conversation with a Giraffe at Dusk in the Zoo" from *Eyes Closed Against the Sun* (Oxford University Press, 1970). "Sunstrike" from *Sjambok and Other Poems* (Oxford University Press, 1964).

ROBERT LOWELL, b. 1917. "Dunbarton" reprinted with the permission of Farrar, Straus & Giroux, Inc. from *Life Studies*, copyright © 1956, 1959 by Robert Lowell.

EDWARD LUCIE-SMITH, b. 1933. "Imperialists in Retirement" from *Confessions and Histories* (Oxford University Press, 1964). "The Lesson" from *A Tropical Childhood and Other Poems* (Oxford University Press, 1961).

GEORGE MACBETH, b. 1932. "Bedtime Story" from *The Broken Places* (Scorpion Press, 1963). "Owl" from *A Doomsday Book* (Scorpion Press, 1965).

NORMAN MACCAIG, b. 1910. "Uncle Roderick" from *A Man in My Position*. All rights reserved. Reprinted by permission of Wesleyan University Press. "Aunt Julia" from *Rings on a Tree*. All rights reserved. Reprinted by permission of Wesleyan University Press.

LOUIS MACNEICE, 1907–1963. "June Thunder," "Prayer before Birth," "The Slow Starter," and "The Streets of Laredo" from *The Collected Poems of Louis MacNeice*, edited by E. R. Dodds. Copyright © The Estate of Louis MacNeice 1966. Reprinted by permission of Oxford University Press, Inc.

CHRISTOPHER MIDDLETON, b. 1926. "For a Junior School Poetry Book" from *Nonsequences, Selfpoems*. By permission of W. W. Norton & Co., Inc. Copyright © 1961, 1962, 1963, 1964, 1965 by Christopher Middleton.

EDWIN MORGAN, b. 1920. "An Addition to the Family: for M.L.," "The Computer's First Christmas Card," "French Persian Cats having a Ball," and "Trio" from *The Second Life* (Edinburgh: Edinburgh University Press, 1968); copyright © 1968 by Edwin Morgan and Edinburgh University Press.

RICHARD MURPHY, b. 1927. "Sailing to an Island" reprinted by permission of Faber and Faber Ltd. from *Sailing to an Island* (1963).

HOWARD NEMEROV, b. 1920. "Grace to be said at the Supermarket" from *The Blue Swallows*, copyright by Howard Nemerov, 1967. "Life Cycle of Common Man" from *New and Selected Poems*, copyright by the University of Chicago, 1960.

NORMAN NICHOLSON, b. 1914. "Cleator Moor" reprinted by permission of Faber & Faber Ltd. from *Five Rivers* (1944). "Rising Five" and "Weather Ear" from *The Pot Geranium* (Faber & Faber Ltd., 1954).

Ltd., 1963); originally in *An Acre of Land* (1952). "For the Record" from *Pieta* (Rupert Hart-Davis Ltd., 1966).

ANTHONY THWAITE, b. 1930. "A Sense of Property" and "Disturbances" from *The Owl in the Tree* (Oxford University Press, 1963). "At Dunwich" from *The Stones of Emptiness* (Oxford University Press, 1967); originally in *New Poems* (1965).

HENRY TREECE, 1912–1966. "Conquerors" reprinted by permission of Faber & Faber Ltd. from *The Haunted Garden* (1947).

VERNON WATKINS, 1906–1967. "The Collier" from *Selected Poems*. Copyright © Faber & Faber, Ltd., 1941, 1948, 1967. Reprinted by permission of New Directions Publishing Corporation.

RICHARD WILBUR, b. 1921. "A Christmas Hymn" from *Advice to a Prophet,* © 1961 by Richard Wilbur. Reprinted by permission of Harcourt Brace Jovanovich, Inc.

JUDITH WRIGHT, b. 1915. "Eve to her Daughters" from *The Other Half* (Angus & Robertson Ltd., 1967).

Contents

Foreword

There are many possible starting points for a modern verse anthology besides the one which I have chosen. A case could be made for beginning with Thomas Hardy or Gerard Manley Hopkins or W. B. Yeats or T. S. Eliot, all of whom were born in the nineteenth century but whose work has helped to shape the poetry of the present. Alternatively it would be reasonable to choose the beginning or end of World War I or II, or to start with any of at least half a dozen poetic "new waves" of the twentieth century. On more mechanical principles it would be possible to begin with the year 1900 or any round number from then until (say) 1960.

I decided to open with the work of poets who were young in the thirties, mainly because (to me at least) this seems to be the point at which poetry begins to speak in our own tones of voice. The poets of the thirties were too young to look back to the old and apparently settled order of things which had ended with the first war. Their eyes were on the social and political ills of their own time, and they looked ahead to the second war which they rightly believed to be on the way. Most of them are still alive, so this is essentially a selection of the work of living writers. And a time span of forty years, I felt, was just long enough to allow some perspective, some sense of change in poetic vision and preoccupations, to emerge. To begin much later and restrict myself to an even shorter time span would have resulted in an elbow-to-elbow jostle of contemporary material in which it would be hard to see any shape.

The arrangement of an anthology is always a problem. Probably the most usual way is under subject headings: love poems, animal poems, poems of place and so on. This has advantages, but I decided that it would be a mistake in this case. Chopping up the contents in such a way would have removed that sense of the passage of time that I wanted to convey. An arrangement in order of the poets' dates of birth would have been logical, but seemed dull and impersonal. I settled in the end for a rough approximation to the order in which the poems were written, modified by a certain amount of shuffling around in order to bring comparable or contrasting poems together, or to produce a more pleasing sequence. My division into sections is intended mainly to provide the reader with some resting places; it is neither strictly according to subject nor strictly chronological.

It seemed to me, for instance, that poems of World War II formed a natural group; and I moved into that group a few poems which were about the war although written later, while moving out of it two or three poems of the war years that were obviously not war poems. In general it can be assumed that poems near the beginning of the book were written early in my period, those in the middle were written in the middle of it, and those at the end are among the most recent; but no more precise conclusions should be drawn from the arrangement. Dates of first known publication in book form are given in the Sources and Acknowledgments. Even this is not an exact guide, however, as poems may remain unpublished, or published only in periodicals, for years before they appear in a book.

I find that, although it was not my intention when I started work, I have chosen mainly poems by people who were young, or youngish, at the time when they were written. Nearly three quarters of these poems were produced by men and women in their twenties and thirties. While many poets continue to develop in their later years, it frequently seems that there is a vigor in a man's early work which he is unable to sustain. If this has turned out to be a young poets' anthology I am not too sorry.

I find also — and again it was not my original intention — that something like half the poems I have chosen have been published in the last ten years. This does not mean that I think the poetry of the 1960s was better than that of the earlier decades. I think rather that perspective has once more asserted itself, this time unconsciously. From where I stand at the time of compiling this anthology, the sixties are still in the foreground, while the fifties, forties and thirties shade away into the middle distance. Moreover, the passage of time brings perspectives of its own. I would expect most of the poems from the thirties in this book still to be strong candidates for an anthology compiled in the year 2000, whereas there would be a much higher wastage among those of the sixties. Much of the recent "popular" poetry—like much of the mass of war poetry that suddenly appeared in the early forties—is interesting and attractive but is not likely, or even intended, to last for a long time.

The few notes that appear with the poems were in the original editions from which I took them, and presumably were written or approved by the poets. I have not supplied any notes of my own. I don't like editors' notes. They smack of the examination room. They imply also that the poem cannot stand up on its own and needs the crutch of explanatory prose. A poem should be allowed, and should be able, to make its own statement. If I have felt that a poem could not achieve its impact without explanation I have preferred to leave it out. Of course there are poems which will offer *more* to the person who has background knowledge or takes the trouble to acquire it. But we are misled if we suppose that notes will ever take us to the heart of a poem. Nobody understands the processes by which a poem is composed or received. Poems that are simply worded and have no obscure allusions may be every bit as profound and mysterious as those that are obviously complicated. I could not, even if I wished, say what every poem in this book is "about." It has been pointed out before now that if the essence of a poem could be conveyed in prose, there would be no need to write the poem.

There are many good poets whose work does not appear in this book, while others of less weight are included. I have not tried to collect the "best" poems of the last forty years, and I have not put any poem in because I felt I ought to do so. (Nor, for that matter, have I left any poem out because it has been too often anthologized already.)

In fact the only reason why I have included any poem in this book is that I like it. And that, I believe, is the best of all reasons. An anthology is a personal thing; that is what gives it its flavor. Nobody, I hope, wants an anthology that looks as if it had been assembled by a computer. If an editor doesn't please himself he doesn't deserve to please anyone. At least I can say I have pleased myself. In fact I have enjoyed myself enormously. All I have left to wish is that my delight will be shared as widely as possible.

J.R.T.
KNUTSFORD, ENGLAND

On This Island

Look, stranger, on this island now
The leaping light for your delight discovers,
Stand stable here
And silent be,
That through the channels of the ear
May wander like a river
The swaying sound of the sea.

Here at the small field's ending pause
When the chalk wall falls to the foam and its tall ledges
Oppose the pluck
And knock of the tide,
And the shingle scrambles after the suck-
ing surf,
And the gull lodges
A moment on its sheer side.

Far off like floating seed the ships
Diverge on urgent voluntary errands,
And the full view
Indeed may enter
And move in memory as now these clouds do,
That pass the harbour mirror
And all the summer through the water saunter.

W. H. AUDEN

Dorset

Rime Intrinsica, Fontmell Magna, Sturminster
    Newton and Melbury Bubb
Whist upon whist upon whist upon whist drive, in
    Institute, Legion and Social Club.
Horny hands that hold the aces which this morning
    held the plough
While Tranter Reuben, T. S. Eliot, H. G. Wells and
    Edith Sitwell lie in Mellstock Churchyard now.

Lord's Day bells from Bingham's Melcombe, Iwerne
    Minster, Shroton, Plush,
Down the grass between the beeches, mellow in the
    evening hush.
Gloved the hands that hold the hymn book, which this
    morning milked the cow
While Tranter Reuben, Mary Borden, Brian Howard and
    Harold Acton lie in Mellstock Churchyard now.

Light's abode, celestial Salem! Lamps of evening,
    smelling strong,
Gleaming on the pitch pine waiting almost empty
    evensong;
From the aisles each window smiles on grave and grass
    and yew tree bough,
While Tranter Reuben, Gordon Selfridge, Edna Best and
    Thomas Hardy lie in Mellstock Churchyard now.

Note: The names in the last lines of these stanzas are not put in out of
malice or satire but merely for their euphony.

JOHN BETJEMAN

The Express

After the first powerful, plain manifesto
The black statement of pistons, without more fuss
But gliding like a queen, she leaves the station.
Without bowing and with restrained unconcern
She passes the houses which humbly crowd outside,
The gasworks, and at last the heavy page
Of death, printed by gravestones in the cemetery.
Beyond the town, there lies the open country
Where, gathering speed, she acquires mystery,
The luminous self-possession of ships on ocean.
It is now she begins to sing—at first quite low
Then loud, and at last with a jazzy madness—
The song of her whistle screaming at curves,
Of deafening tunnels, brakes, innumerable bolts.
And always light, aerial, underneath,
Retreats the elate metre of her wheels.
Steaming through metal landscape on her lines
She plunges new eras of white happiness
Where speed throws up strange shapes, broad curves
And parallels clean like trajectories from guns.
At last, further than Edinburgh or Rome,
Beyond the crest of the world, she reaches night
Where only a low stream-line brightness
Of phosphorus on the tossing hills is light.
Ah, like a comet through flame, she moves entranced
Wrapt in her music no bird song, no, nor bough
Breaking with honey buds, shall ever equal.

STEPHEN SPENDER

Moving through the silent crowd

Moving through the silent crowd
Who stand behind dull cigarettes
These men who idle in the road,
I have the sense of falling light.

They lounge at corners of the street
And greet friends with a shrug of shoulder
And turn their empty pockets out,
The cynical gestures of the poor.

Now they've no work, like better men
Who sit at desks and take much pay
They sleep long nights and rise at ten
To watch the hours that drain away.

I'm jealous of the weeping hours
They stare through with such hungry eyes.
I'm haunted by these images,
I'm haunted by their emptiness.

STEPHEN SPENDER

La Marche
des Machines

This piston's infinite recurrence is
night morning night and morning night and
death and birth and death and birth and this
crank climbs (blind Sisyphus) and see

steel teeth greet
bow deliberate
delicately lace
in lethal kiss
       God's teeth bite whitely tight

slowly the gigantic oh slowly the steel spine dislocates

wheels grazing (accurately missing) waltz

two cranes do a hundred-ton tango against the sky

A. S. J. TESSIMOND

23

The Collier

When I was born on Amman hill
A dark bird crossed the sun.
Sharp on the floor the shadow fell;
I was the youngest son.

And when I went to the County School
I worked in a shaft of light.
In the wood of the desk I cut my name:
Dai for Dynamite.

The tall black hills my brothers stood;
Their lessons all were done.
From the door of the school when I ran out
They frowned to watch me run.

The slow grey bells they rung a chime
Surly with grief or age.
Clever or clumsy, lad or lout,
All would look for a wage.

I learnt the valley flowers' names
And the rough bark knew my knees.
I brought home trout from the river
And spotted eggs from the trees.

A coloured coat I was given to wear
Where the lights of the rough land shone.
Still jealous of my favour
The tall black hills looked on.

They dipped my coat in the blood of a kid
And they cast me down a pit,
And although I crossed with strangers
There was no way up from it.

Soon as I went from the County School
I worked in a shaft. Said Jim,
'You will get your chain of gold, my lad,
But not for a likely time.'

And one said, 'Jack was not raised up
When the wind blew out the light
Though he interpreted their dreams
And guessed their fears by night.'

And Tom, he shivered his leper's lamp
For the stain that round him grew;
And I heard mouths pray in the after-damp
When the picks would not break through.

They changed words there in darkness
And still through my head they run,
And white on my limbs is the linen sheet
And gold on my neck the sun.

VERNON WATKINS

An Elementary School Class Room in a Slum

Far far from gusty waves, these children's faces.
Like rootless weeds the torn hair round their
    paleness.
The tall girl with her weighed-down head. The paper-
seeming boy with rat's eyes. The stunted unlucky heir
Of twisted bones, reciting a father's gnarled disease,
His lesson from his desk. At back of the dim class,
One unnoted, sweet and young: his eyes live in a
    dream
Of squirrels' game, in tree room, other than this.

On sour cream walls, donations. Shakespeare's head
Cloudless at dawn, civilized dome riding all cities.
Belled, flowery, Tyrolese valley. Open-handed map
Awarding the world its world. And yet, for these
Children, these windows, not this world, are world,
Where all their future's painted with a fog,
A narrow street sealed in with a lead sky,
Far far from rivers, capes, and stars of words.

Surely Shakespeare is wicked, the map a bad example
With ships and sun and love tempting them to steal—
For lives that slyly turn in their cramped holes
From fog to endless night? On their slag heap, these
    children
Wear skins peeped through by bones and spectacles
    of steel
With mended glass, like bottle bits on stones.
All of their time and space are foggy slum
So blot their maps with slums as big as doom.

Unless, governor, teacher, inspector, visitor,
This map becomes their window and these windows
That open on their lives like crouching tombs
Break, O break open, till they break the town
And show the children to the fields and all their world
Azure on their sands, to let their tongues
Run naked into books, the white and green leaves
    open
The history theirs whose language is the sun.

STEPHEN SPENDER

Carol

There was a Boy bedded in bracken,
Like to a sleeping snake all curled he lay,
On his thin navel turned this spinning sphere,
Each feeble finger fetched seven suns away,
He was not dropped in good-for-lambing weather,
He took no suck when shook buds sing together,
But he is come in cold-as-workhouse weather,
   Poor as a Salford child.

JOHN SHORT

O what is that sound

O what is that sound which so thrills the ear
   Down in the valley drumming, drumming?
Only the scarlet soldiers, dear,
   The soldiers coming.

O what is that light I see flashing so clear
   Over the distance brightly, brightly?
Only the sun on their weapons, dear,
   As they step lightly.

O what are they doing with all that gear,
   What are they doing this morning, this morning?
Only their usual manœuvres, dear,
   Or perhaps a warning.

O why have they left the road down there,
   Why are they suddenly wheeling, wheeling?
Perhaps a change in their orders, dear.
   Why are you kneeling?

O haven't they stopped for the doctor's care,
   Haven't they reined their horses, their horses?
Why, they are none of them wounded, dear,
   None of these forces.

O is it the parson they want, with white hair,
   Is it the parson, is it, is it?
No, they are passing his gateway, dear,
   Without a visit.

O it must be the farmer who lives so near.
   It must be the farmer so cunning, so cunning?
They have passed the farmyard already, dear,
   And now they are running.

O where are you going? Stay with me here!
  Were the vows you swore deceiving, deceiving?
No, I promised to love you, dear,
  But I must be leaving.

O it's broken the lock and splintered the door,
  O it's the gate where they're turning, turning;
Their boots are heavy on the floor
  And their eyes are burning.

W. H. AUDEN

Musée des Beaux Arts

About suffering they were never wrong,
The Old Masters: how well they understood
Its human position; how it takes place
While someone else is eating or opening a window or just
    walking dully along;
How, when the aged are reverently, passionately waiting
For the miraculous birth, there always must be
Children who did not specially want it to happen, skating
On a pond at the edge of the wood:
They never forgot
That even the dreadful martyrdom must run its course
Anyhow in a corner, some untidy spot
Where the dogs go on with their doggy life and the torturer's
    horse
Scratches its innocent behind on a tree.

In Breughel's *Icarus*, for instance: how everything turns
    away
Quite leisurely from the disaster; the ploughman may
Have heard the splash, the forsaken cry,
But for him it was not an important failure; the sun shone
As it had to on the white legs disappearing into the green
Water; and the expensive delicate ship that must have seen
Something amazing, a boy falling out of the sky,
Had somewhere to get to and sailed calmly on.

W. H. AUDEN

The Fox

Because the snow is deep
Without spot that white falling through white air

Because she limps a little—bleeds
Where they shot her

Because hunters have guns
And dogs have hangmen's legs

Because I'd like to take her in my arms
And tend her wound

Because she can't afford to die
Killing the young in her belly

I don't know what to say of a soldier's dying
Because there are no proportions in death.

KENNETH PATCHEN

Ultima Ratio Regum

The guns spell money's ultimate reason
In letters of lead on the spring hillside.
But the boy lying dead under the olive trees
Was too young and too silly
To have been notable to their important eye.
He was a better target for a kiss.

When he lived, tall factory hooters never summoned
    him.
Nor did restaurant plate-glass doors revolve to wave
    him in.
His name never appeared in the papers.
The world maintained its traditional wall
Round the dead with their gold sunk deep as a well,
Whilst his life, intangible as a Stock Exchange
    rumour, drifted outside.

O too lightly he threw down his cap
One day when the breeze threw petals from the trees.
The unflowering wall sprouted with guns,
Machine-gun anger quickly scythed the grasses;
Flags and leaves fell from hands and branches;
The tweed cap rotted in the nettles.

Consider his life which was valueless
In terms of employment, hotel ledgers, news files.
Consider. One bullet in ten thousand kills a man.
Ask. Was so much expenditure justified
On the death of one so young and so silly
Lying under the olive trees, O world, O death?

ultima ratio regum: the final argument of kings.

STEPHEN SPENDER

And death
shall have no dominion

And death shall have no dominion.
Dead men naked they shall be one
With the man in the wind and the west moon;
When their bones are picked clean and the clean bones gone,
They shall have stars at elbow and foot;
Though they go mad they shall be sane,
Though they sink through the sea they shall rise again;
Though lovers be lost love shall not;
And death shall have no dominion.

And death shall have no dominion.
Under the windings of the sea
They lying long shall not die windily;
Twisting on racks when sinews give way,
Strapped to a wheel, yet they shall not break;
Faith in their hands shall snap in two,
And the unicorn evils run them through;
Split all ends up they shan't crack;
And death shall have no dominion.

And death shall have no dominion.
No more may gulls cry at their ears
Or waves break loud on the seashores;
Where blew a flower may a flower no more
Lift its head to the blows of the rain;
Though they be mad and dead as nails,
Heads of the characters hammer through daisies;
Break in the sun till the sun breaks down,
And death shall have no dominion.

DYLAN THOMAS

June Thunder

The Junes were free and full, driving through tiny
Roads, the mudguards brushing the cowparsley,
Through fields of mustard and under boldly embattled
    Mays and chestnuts.

Or between beeches verdurous and voluptuous
Or where broom and gorse beflagged the chalkland—
All the flare and gusto of the unenduring
    Joys of a season

Now returned but I note as more appropriate
To the maturer mood impending thunder
With an indigo sky and the garden hushed except for
    The treetops moving.

Then the curtains in my room blow suddenly inward,
The shrubbery rustles, birds fly heavily homeward,
The white flowers fade to nothing on the trees and rain
    comes
    Down like a dropscene.

Now there comes the catharsis, the cleansing downpour
Breaking the blossoms of our overdated fancies
Our old sentimentality and whimsicality
    Loves of the morning.

Blackness at half-past eight, the night's precursor,
Clouds like falling masonry and lightning's lavish
Annunciation, the sword of the mad archangel
    Flashed from the scabbard.

If only you would come and dare the crystal
Rampart of rain and the bottomless moat of thunder,
If only you would come I should be happy
    Now if now only.

LOUIS MACNEICE

Snow in Europe

Out of their slumber Europeans spun
Dense dreams: appeasement, miracle, glimpsed flash
Of a new golden era; but could not restrain
The vertical white weight that fell last night
And made their continent a blank.

Hush, says the sameness of the snow
The Ural and the Jura now rejoin
The furthest Arctic's desolation. All is one;
Sheer monotone: plain, mountain; country, town:
Contours and boundaries no longer show.

The warring flags hang colourless a while;
Now midnight's icy zero feigns a truce
Between the sighs and seasons, and fades out
All shots and cries. But when the great thaw comes,
How red shall be the melting snow, how loud the drums!

DAVID GASCOYNE

Watching Post

A hill flank overlooking the Axe valley.
Among the stubble a farmer and I keep watch
For whatever may come to injure our countryside—
Light-signals, parachutes, bombs, or sea-invaders.
The moon looks over the hill's shoulder, and hope
Mans the old ramparts of an English night.

In a house down there was Marlborough born. One night
Monmouth marched to his ruin out of that valley.
Beneath our castled hill, where Britons kept watch,
Is a church where the Drakes, old lords of this country-
    side,
Sleep under their painted effigies. No invaders
Can dispute their legacy of toughness and hope.

Two counties away, over Bristol, the searchlights hope
To find what danger is in the air tonight.
Presently gunfire from Portland reaches our valley
Tapping like an ill-hung door in a draught. My watch
Says nearly twelve. All over the countryside
Moon-dazzled men are peering out for invaders.

The farmer and I talk for a while of invaders:
But soon we turn to crops—the annual hope,
Making of cider, prizes for ewes. Tonight
How many hearts along this war-mazed valley
Dream of a day when at peace they may work and watch
The small sufficient wonders of the countryside.

Image or fact, we both in the countryside
Have found our natural law, and until invaders
Come will answer its need: for both of us, hope
Means a harvest from small beginnings, who this night
While the moon sorts out into shadow and shape our valley,
A farmer and a poet, are keeping watch.

C. DAY LEWIS

Naming of Parts

Today we have naming of parts. Yesterday,
We had daily cleaning. And tomorrow morning,
We shall have what to do after firing. But today,
Today we have naming of parts. Japonica
Glistens like coral in all of the neighbouring gardens,
    And today we have naming of parts.

This is the lower sling swivel. And this
Is the upper sling swivel, whose use you will see,
When you are given your slings. And this is the piling swivel,
Which in your case you have not got. The branches
Hold in the gardens their silent, eloquent gestures,
    Which in our case we have not got.

This is the safety-catch, which is always released
With an easy flick of the thumb. And please do not let me
See anyone using his finger. You can do it quite easy
If you have any strength in your thumb. The blossoms
Are fragile and motionless, never letting anyone see
    Any of them using their finger.

And this you can see is the bolt. The purpose of this
Is to open the breech, as you see. We can slide it
Rapidly backwards and forwards: we call this
Easing the spring. And rapidly backwards and forwards
The early bees are assaulting and fumbling the flowers:
    They call it easing the Spring.

They call it easing the Spring: it is perfectly easy
If you have any strength in your thumb: like the bolt,
And the breech, and the cocking-piece, and the point of
    balance,
Which in our case we have not got; and the almond-
    blossom
Silent in all of the gardens and the bees going backwards
    and forwards,
    For today we have naming of parts.

HENRY REED

Unseen Fire

This is a damned inhuman sort of war.
I have been fighting in a dressing-gown
Most of the night; I cannot see the guns,
The sweating gun-detachments or the planes;

I sweat down here before a symbol thrown
Upon a screen, sift facts, initiate
Swift calculations and swift orders; wait
For the precise split-second to order fire.

We chant our ritual words; beyond the phones
A ghost repeats the orders to the guns:
One Fire . . . Two Fire . . . ghosts answer: the guns roar
Abruptly; and an aircraft waging war
Inhumanly from nearly five miles height
Meets our bouquet of death—and turns sharp right.

*　　*　　*　　*　　*

This is a damned unnatural sort of war;
The pilot sits among the clouds, quite sure
About the values he is fighting for;
He cannot hear beyond his veil of sound,

He cannot see the people on the ground;
He only knows that on the sloping map
Of sea-fringed town and country people creep
Like ants—and who cares if ants laugh or weep?

To us he is no more than a machine
Shown on an instrument; what can he mean
In human terms?—a man, somebody's son,
Proud of his skill; compact of flesh and bone
Fragile as Icarus—and our desire
To see that damned machine come down on fire.

R. N. CURREY

For the Record

What was your war record, Prytherch?
I know: up and down the same field,
Following a horse; no oil for tractors;
Sniped at by rain, but never starving.
Did you listen to the reports
Of how heroes are fashioned and how killed?
Did you wait up for the news?
Your world was the same world as before
Wars were contested, noisier only
Because of the echoes in the sky.
The blast worried your hair on its way to the hill;
The distances were a wound
Opened each night. Yet in your acres,
With no medals to be won,
You were on the old side of life,
Helping it in through the dark door
Of earth and beast, quietly repairing
The rents of history with your hands.

R. S. THOMAS

43

Cleator Moor

From one shaft at Cleator Moor
They mined for coal and iron ore.
This harvest below ground could show
Black and red currants on one tree.

In furnaces they burnt the coal,
The ore they smelted into steel,
And railway lines from end to end
Corseted the bulging land.

Pylons sprouted on the fells,
Stakes were driven in like nails,
And the ploughed fields of Devonshire
Were sliced with the steel of Cleator Moor.

The land waxed fat and greedy too,
It would not share the fruits it grew,
And coal and ore, as sloe and plum,
Lay black and red for jamming time.

The pylons rusted on the fells,
The gutters leaked beside the walls,
The women searched the ebb-tide tracks
For knobs of coal and broken sticks.

But now the pits are wick with men,
Digging like dogs dig for a bone:
For food and life *we* dig the earth—
In Cleator Moor they dig for death.

Every wagon of cold coal
Is fire to drive a turbine wheel;
Every knuckle of soft ore
A bullet in a soldier's ear.

The miner at the rockface stands,
With his segged and bleeding hands
Heaps on his head the fiery coal,
And feels the iron in his soul.

NORMAN NICHOLSON

The Streets of Laredo

O early one morning I walked out like Agag,
Early one morning to walk through the fire
Dodging the pythons that leaked on the pavements
With tinkle of glasses and tangle of wire;

When grimed to the eyebrows I met an old fireman
Who looked at me wryly and thus did he say:
'The streets of Laredo are closed to all traffic,
We won't never master this joker today.

'O hold the branch tightly and wield the axe brightly,
The bank is in powder, the banker's in hell,
But loot is still free on the streets of Laredo
And when we drive home we drive home on the bell.'

Then out from a doorway there sidled a cockney,
A rocking-chair rocking on top of his head:
'O fifty-five years I been feathering my love-nest
And look at it now—why, you'd sooner be dead.'

At which there arose from a wound in the asphalt,
His big wig a-smoulder, Sir Christopher Wren
Saying: 'Let them make hay of the streets of Laredo;
When your ground-rents expire I will build them again.'

Then twanging their bibles with wrath in their nostrils
From Bunhill Fields came Bunyan and Blake:
'Laredo the golden is fallen, is fallen;
Your flame shall not quench nor your thirst shall not slake.'

'I come to Laredo to find me asylum,'
Says Tom Dick and Harry the Wandering Jew;
'They tell me report at the first police station
But the station is pancaked—so what can I do?'

Thus eavesdropping sadly I strolled through Laredo
Perplexed by the dicta misfortunes inspire
Till one low last whisper inveigled my earhole—
The voice of the Angel, the voice of the fire:

O late, very late, have I come to Laredo
A whimsical bride in my new scarlet dress
But at last I took pity on those who were waiting
To see my regalia and feel my caress.

Now ring the bells gaily and play the hose daily,
Put splints on your legs, put a gag on your breath;
O you streets of Laredo, you streets of Laredo,
Lay down the red carpet—My dowry is death.

LOUIS MACNEICE

The Evacuee

She woke up under a loose quilt
Of leaf patterns, woven by the light
At the small window, busy with the boughs
Of a young cherry; but wearily she lay,
Waiting for the siren, slow to trust
Nature's deceptive peace, and then afraid
Of the long silence, she would have crept
Uneasily from the bedroom with its frieze
Of fresh sunlight, had not a cock crowed,
Shattering the surface of that limpid pool
Of stillness, and before the ripples died
One by one in the field's shallows,
The farm woke with uninhibited din.

And now the noise and not the silence drew her
Down the bare stairs at great speed.
The sounds and voices were a rough sheet
Waiting to catch her, as though she leaped
From a scorched storey of the charred past.

And there the table and the gallery
Of farm faces trying to be kind
Beckoned her nearer, and she sat down
Under an awning of salt hams.

And so she grew, a small bird in the nest
Of welcome that was built about her,
Home now after so long away
In the flowerless streets of the drab town.
The men watched her busy with the hens,
The soft flesh ripening warm as corn
On the sticks of limbs, the grey eyes clear,
Rinsed with dew of their long dread.
The men watched her, and, nodding, smiled
With earth's charity, patient and strong.

R. S. THOMAS

47

A Refusal to Mourn the Death, by Fire, of a Child in London

Never until the mankind making
Bird beast and flower
Fathering and all humbling darkness
Tells with silence the last light breaking
And the still hour
Is coming of the sea tumbling in harness

And I must enter again the round
Zion of the water bead
And the synagogue of the ear of corn
Shall I let pray the shadow of a sound
Or sow my salt seed
In the least valley of sackcloth to mourn

The majesty and burning of the child's death.
I shall not murder
The mankind of her going with a grave truth
Nor blaspheme down the stations of the breath
With any further
Elegy of innocence and youth.

Deep with the first dead lies London's daughter,
Robed in the long friends,
The grains beyond age, the dark veins of her mother,
Secret by the unmourning water
Of the riding Thames.
After the first death, there is no other.

DYLAN THOMAS

48

Carentan O Carentan

Trees in the old days used to stand
And shape a shady lane
Where lovers wandered hand in hand
Who came from Carentan.

This was the shining green canal
Where we came two by two
Walking at combat-interval.
Such trees we never knew.

The day was early June, the ground
Was soft and bright with dew.
Far away the guns did sound,
But here the sky was blue.

The sky was blue, but there a smoke
Hung still above the sea
Where the ships together spoke
To towns we could not see.

Could you have seen us through a glass
You would have said a walk
Of farmers out to turn the grass,
Each with his own hay-fork.

The watchers in their leopard suits
Waited till it was time,
And aimed between the belt and boot
And let the barrel climb.

I must lie down at once, there is
A hammer at my knee.
And call it death or cowardice,
Don't count again on me.

Everything's all right, Mother,
Everyone gets the same
At one time or another.
It's all in the game.

I never strolled, nor ever shall,
Down such a leafy lane.
I never drank in a canal
Nor ever shall again.

There is a whistling in the leaves
And it is not the wind,
The twigs are falling from the knives
That cut men to the ground.

Tell me, Master-Sergeant,
The way to turn and shoot.
But the Sergeant's silent
That taught me how to do it.

O Captain, show us quickly
Our place upon the map.
But the Captain's sickly
And taking a long nap.

Lieutenant, what's my duty,
My place in the platoon?
He too's a sleeping beauty,
Charmed by that strange tune.

Carentan O Carentan
Before we met with you
We never yet had lost a man
Or known what death could do.

LOUIS SIMPSON

50

Conquerors

By sundown we came to a hidden village
Where all the air was still
And no sound met our tired ears, save
For the sorry drip of rain from blackened trees
And the melancholy song of swinging gates.
Then through a broken pane some of us saw
A dead bird in a rusting cage, still
Pressing his thin tattered breast against the bars,
His beak wide open. And
As we hurried through the weed-grown street,
A gaunt dog started up from some dark place
And shambled off on legs as thin as sticks
Into the wood, to die at least in peace.
No-one had told us victory was like this;
Not one amongst us would have eaten bread
Before he'd filled the mouth of the grey child
That sprawled, stiff as a stone, before the shattered
    door.
There was not one who did not think of home.

HENRY TREECE

Prayer before Birth

I am not yet born; O hear me.
Let not the bloodsucking bat or the rat or the stoat or the
   club-footed ghoul come near me.

I am not yet born, console me.
I fear that the human race may with tall walls wall me,
   with strong drugs dope me, with wise lies lure me,
      on black racks rack me, in blood-baths roll me.

I am not yet born; provide me
With water to dandle me, grass to grow for me, trees to talk
   to me, sky to sing to me, birds and a white light
      in the back of my mind to guide me.

I am not yet born; forgive me
For the sins that in me the world shall commit, my words
   when they speak me, my thoughts when they think me,
      my treason engendered by traitors beyond me,
         my life when they murder by means of my
            hands, my death when they live me.

I am not yet born; rehearse me
In the parts I must play and the cues I must take when
   old men lecture me, bureaucrats hector me, mountains
      frown at me, lovers laugh at me, the white
         waves call me to folly and the desert calls
            me to doom and the beggar refuses
               my gift and my children curse me.

I am not yet born; O hear me,
Let not the man who is beast or who thinks he is God
   come near me.

I am not yet born; O fill me
With strength against those who would freeze my
    humanity, would dragoon me into a lethal automaton,
        would make me a cog in a machine, a thing with
            one face, a thing, and against all those
                who would dissipate my entirety, would
                    blow me like thistledown hither and
                        thither or hither and thither
                            like water held in the
                                hands would spill me.

Let them not make me a stone and let them not spill me.
Otherwise kill me.

LOUIS MACNEICE

Poem in October

It was my thirtieth year to heaven
Woke to my hearing from harbour and neighbour wood
And the mussel pooled and the heron
    Priested shore
    The morning beckon
With water praying and call of seagull and rook
And the knock of sailing boats on the net webbed wall
    Myself to set foot
      That second
In the still sleeping town and set forth.

My birthday began with the water-
Birds and the birds of the winged trees flying my name
Above the farms and the white horses
    And I rose
    In rainy autumn
And walked abroad in a shower of all my days.
High tide and the heron dived when I took the road
    Over the border
    And the gates
Of the town closed as the town awoke.

A springful of larks in a rolling
Cloud and the roadside bushes brimming with whistling
Blackbirds and the sun of October
    Summery
    On the hill's shoulder,
Here were fond climates and sweet singers suddenly
Come in the morning where I wandered and listened
    To the rain wringing
      Wind blow cold
In the wood faraway under me.

Pale rain over the dwindling harbour
And over the sea wet church the size of a snail
With its horns through mist and the castle

Brown as owls
But all the gardens
Of spring and summer were blooming in the tall tales
Beyond the border and under the lark full cloud.
There could I marvel
My birthday
Away but the weather turned around.

It turned away from the blithe country
And down the other air and the blue altered sky
Streamed again a wonder of summer
With apples
Pears and red currants
And I saw in the turning so clearly a child's
Forgotten mornings when he walked with his mother
Through the parables
Of sun light
And the legends of the green chapels

And the twice told fields of infancy
That his tears burned my cheeks and his heart moved in mine.
These were the woods the river and sea
Where a boy
In the listening
Summertime of the dead whispered the truth of his joy
To the trees and the stones and the fish in the tide.
And the mystery
Sang alive
Still in the water and singingbirds.

And there could I marvel my birthday
Away but the weather turned around. And the true
Joy of the long dead child sang burning
In the sun.
It was my thirtieth
Year to heaven stood there then in the summer noon
Though the town below lay leaved with October blood.
O may my heart's truth
Still be sung
On this high hill in a year's turning.

DYLAN THOMAS

Milkmaid

The girl's far treble, muted to the heat,
calls like a fainting bird across the fields
to where her flock lies panting for her voice,
their black horns buried deep in marigolds.

They climbed awake, like drowsy butterflies,
and press their red flanks through the tall branched grass,
and as they go their wandering tongues embrace
the vacant summer mirrored in their eyes.

Led to the limestone shadows of a barn
they snuff their past embalmèd in the hay,
while her cool hand, cupped to the udder's fount,
distils the brimming harvest of their day.

Look what a cloudy cream the earth gives out,
fat juice of buttercups and meadow-rye;
the girl dreams milk within her body's field
and hears, far off, her muted children cry.

LAURIE LEE

April Rise

If ever I saw blessing in the air
  I see it now in this still early day
Where lemon-green the vaporous morning drips
  Wet sunlight on the powder of my eye.

Blown bubble-film of blue, the sky wraps round
  Weeds of warm light whose every root and rod
Splutters with soapy green, and all the world
  Sweats with the bead of summer in its bud.

If ever I heard blessing it is there
  Where birds in trees that shoals and shadows are
Splash with their hidden wings and drops of sound
  Break on my ears their crests of throbbing air.

Pure in the haze the emerald sun dilates,
  The lips of sparrows milk the mossy stones,
While white as water by the lake a girl
  Swims her green hand among the gathered swans.

Now, as the almond burns its smoking wick,
  Dropping small flames to light the candled grass;
Now, as my low blood scales its second chance,
  If ever world were blessèd, now it is.

LAURIE LEE

Welsh Landscape

To live in Wales is to be conscious
At dusk of the spilled blood
That went to the making of the wild sky,
Dyeing the immaculate rivers
In all their courses.
It is to be aware,
Above the noisy tractor
And hum of the machine
Of strife in the strung woods,
Vibrant with sped arrows.
You cannot live in the present,
At least not in Wales.
There is the language for instance,
The soft consonants
Strange to the ear.
There are cries in the dark at night
As owls answer the moon,
And thick ambush of shadows,
Hushed at the fields' corners.
There is no present in Wales,
And no future;
There is only the past,
Brittle with relics,
Wind-bitten towers and castles
With sham ghosts;
Mouldering quarries and mines;
And an impotent people,
Sick with inbreeding,
Worrying the carcase of an old song.

R. S. THOMAS

Goodbye

So we must say Goodbye, my darling,
and go, as lovers go, for ever;
Tonight remains, to pack and fix on labels
And make an end of lying down together.

I put a final shilling in the gas,
And watch you slip your dress below your knees
And lie so still I hear your rustling comb
Modulate the autumn in the trees.

And all the countless things I shall remember
Lay mummy-cloths of silence round my head;
I fill the carafe with a drink of water;
You say 'We paid a guinea for this bed,'

And then, 'We'll leave some gas, a little warmth
For the next resident, and these dry flowers,'
And turn your face away, afraid to speak
The big word, that Eternity is ours.

Your kisses close my eyes and yet you stare
As though God struck a child with nameless fears;
Perhaps the water glitters and discloses
Time's chalice and its limpid useless tears.

Everything we renounce except our selves;
Selfishness is the last of all to go;
Our sighs are exhalations of the earth,
Our footprints leave a track across the snow.

We made the universe to be our home,
Our nostrils took the wind to be our breath,
Our hearts are massive towers of delight,
We stride across the seven seas of death.

Yet when all's done you'll keep the emerald
I placed upon your finger in the street;
And I will keep the patches that you sewed
On my old battledress tonight, my sweet.

ALUN LEWIS

The Hill Farmer Speaks

I am the farmer, stripped of love
And thought and grace by the land's hardness;
But what I am saying over the fields'
Desolate acres, rough with dew,
Is, Listen, listen, I am a man like you.

The wind goes over the hill pastures
Year after year, and the ewes starve,
Milkless, for want of the new grass.
And I starve, too, for something the spring
Can never foster in veins run dry.

The pig is a friend, the cattle's breath
Mingles with mine in the still lanes;
I wear it willingly like a cloak
To shelter me from your curious gaze.

The hens go in and out at the door
From sun to shadow, as stray thoughts pass
Over the floor of my wide skull.
The dirt is under my cracked nails;
The tale of my life is smirched with dung;
The phlegm rattles. But what I am saying
Over the grasses rough with dew
Is, Listen, listen, I am a man like you.

R. S. THOMAS

Cynddylan on a Tractor

Ah, you should see Cynddylan on a tractor.
Gone the old look that yoked him to the soil;
He's a new man now, part of the machine,
His nerves of metal and his blood oil.
The clutch curses, but the gears obey
His least bidding, and lo, he's away
Out of the farmyard, scattering hens.
Riding to work now as a great man should,
He is the knight at arms breaking the fields'
Mirror of silence, emptying the wood
Of foxes and squirrels and bright jays.
The sun comes over the tall trees
Kindling all the hedges, but not for him
Who runs his engine on a different fuel.
And all the birds are singing, bills wide in vain,
As Cynddylan passes proudly up the lane.

R. S. THOMAS

If ever you go to Dublin town

If ever you go to Dublin town
In a hundred years or so
Inquire for me in Baggot Street
And what I was like to know.
O he was a queer one,
Fol dol the di do,
He was a queer one
I tell you.

My great-grandmother knew him well,
He asked her to come and call
On him at his flat and she giggled at the thought
Of a young girl's lovely fall.
O he was dangerous,
Fol dol the di do,
He was dangerous
I tell you.

On Pembroke Road look out for my ghost,
Dishevelled with shoes untied,
Playing through the railings with little children
Whose children have long since died.
O he was a nice man,
Fol dol the di do,
He was a nice man
I tell you.

Go into a pub and listen well
If my voice still echoes there,
Ask the men what their grandsires thought
And tell them to answer fair.
O he was eccentric,
Fol dol the di do,
He was eccentric
I tell you.

He had the knack of making men feel
As small as they really were
Which meant as great as God had made them
But as males they disliked his air.
O he was a proud one,
Fol dol the di do,
He was a proud one
I tell you.

If ever you go to Dublin town
In a hundred years or so
Sniff for my personality,
Is it Vanity's vapour now?
O he was a vain one,
Fol dol the di do,
He was a vain one
I tell you.

I saw his name with a hundred others
In a book in the library,
It said he had never fully achieved
His potentiality.
O he was slothful,
Fol dol the di do,
He was slothful
I tell you.

He knew that posterity has no use
For anything but the soul,
The lines that speak the passionate heart,
The spirit that lives alone.
O he was a lone one,
Fol dol the di do,
Yet he lived happily
I tell you.

PATRICK KAVANAGH

The Licorice Fields at Pontefract

In the licorice fields at Pontefract
  My love and I did meet
And many a burdened licorice bush
  Was blooming round our feet;
Red hair she had and golden skin,
Her sulky lips were shaped for sin,
Her sturdy legs were flannel-slack'd,
The strongest legs in Pontefract.

The light and dangling licorice flowers
  Gave off the sweetest smells;
From various black Victorian towers
  The Sunday evening bells
Came pealing over dales and hills
And tanneries and silent mills
And lowly streets where country stops
And little shuttered corner shops.

She cast her blazing eyes on me
  And plucked a licorice leaf;
I was her captive slave and she
  My red-haired robber chief.
Oh love! for love I could not speak,
It left me winded, wilting, weak
And held in brown arms strong and bare
And wound with flaming ropes of hair.

JOHN BETJEMAN

On a Friend's Escape from Drowning off the Norfolk Coast

Came up that cold sea at Cromer like a running grave
    Beside him as he struck
Wildly towards the shore, but the blackcapped wave
    Crossed him and swung him back,
And he saw his son digging in the castled dirt that
        could save.
    Then the farewell rock
Rose a last time to his eyes. As he cried out
    A pawing gag of the sea
Smothered his cry and he sank in his own shout
    Like a dying airman. Then she
Deep near her son asleep on the hourglass sand
    Was awakened by whom
Save the Fate who knew that this was the wrong time:
    And opened her eyes
On the death of her son's begetter. Up she flies
    Into the hydra-headed
Grave as he closes his life upon her who for
    Life has so richly bedded him.
But she drove through his drowning like Orpheus and
    tore
    Back by the hair
Her escaping bridegroom. And on the sand their son
    Stood laughing where
He was almost an orphan. Then the three lay down
    On that cold sand,
Each holding the other by a living hand.

GEORGE BARKER

Weather Ear

Lying in bed in the dark, I hear the bray
Of the furnace hooter rasping the slates, and say:
'The wind will be in the east, and frost on the nose, today.'

Or when, in the still, small, conscience hours, I hear
The market clock-bell clacking close to my ear:
'A north-west wind from the fell, and the sky-light swilled and
    clear.'

But now when the roofs are sulky as the dead,
With a snuffle and sniff in the gullies, a drip on the lead:
'No wind at all, and the street stone-deaf with a cold in the head.'

NORMAN NICHOLSON

Rising Five

'I'm rising five', he said,
'Not four', and little coils of hair
Un–clicked themselves upon his head.
His spectacles, brimful of eyes to stare
At me and the meadow, reflected cones of light
Above his toffee-buckled cheeks. He'd been alive
Fifty-six months or perhaps a week more:

                            not four,
But rising five.

Around him in the field the cells of spring
Bubbled and doubled; buds unbuttoned; shoot
And stem shook out the creases from their frills,
And every tree was swilled with green.
It was the season after blossoming,
Before the forming of the fruit:

                    not May,
But rising June.

        And in the sky
The dust dissected the tangential light:

                      not day,
But rising night;
          not now,
But rising soon.

The new buds push the old leaves from the bough.
We drop our youth behind us like a boy
Throwing away his toffee-wrappers. We never see the flower,
But only the fruit in the flower; never the fruit,
But only the rot in the fruit. We look for the marriage bed
In the baby's cradle, we look for the grave in the bed:

                      not living,
But rising dead.

NORMAN NICHOLSON

Gunpowder Plot

For days these curious cardboard buds have lain
In brightly coloured boxes. Soon the night
Will come. We pray there'll be no sudden rain
To make these magic orchids flame less bright.

Now in the garden's darkness they begin
To flower: the frenzied whizz of Catherine-wheel
Puts forth its fiery petals and the thin
Rocket soars to burst upon the steel

Bulwark of a cloud. And then the guy,
Absurdly human phoenix, is again
Gulped by greedy flames: the harvest sky
Is flecked with threshed and glittering golden grain.

'Uncle! A cannon! Watch me as I light it!'
The women helter-skelter, squealing high,
Retreat; the paper fuse is quickly lit,
A cat-like hiss, and spit of fire, a sly

Falter, then the air is shocked with blast.
The cannon bangs and in my nostrils drifts
A bitter scent that brings the lurking past
Lurching to my side. The present shifts,

Allows a ten-year memory to walk
Unhindered now; and so I'm forced to hear
The banshee howl of mortar and the talk
Of men who died, am forced to taste my fear.

I listen for a moment to the guns,
The torn earth's grunts, recalling how I prayed.
The past retreats. I hear a corpse's sons—
'Who's scared of bangers!' 'Uncle! John's afraid!'

VERNON SCANNELL

Aunts Watching Television

The aunts who knew not Africa
But spoke of having been to Weymouth in the spring—
Not last spring but the year the lilac was so good—
Who never saw prize-fighters in a ring,
But could recall a fox-hunt in the neighbourhood.

Two aunts who never went abroad,
Nor travelled far in love, nor were much wronged, nor sinned
A lot—but for such peccadillos as to damn,
With tiny oaths, late frost or some chill wind,
Slugs at the dahlias or wasps at homemade jam.

Two aunts who, after silences,
Spoke knowingly of angels passing overhead:
But who prayed little and slept well, were worried less
By death than weeds: but hoped to die in bed,
Untouched by magic or by economic stress.

This age's beneficiaries
For whom our century endows this box of dreams,
Conferring prize-fighters, dancers of unimaginable grace,
Glimpses of Africa, of football teams,
Of statesmen, of the finish of a classic race.

Vestals of the impalpable,
Dazed by its prodigality, by acrobats
On bicycles, by lovers speaking Shakespeare's lines,
Mazed by murders, by speeches from democrats,
Wooed by cooking hints and the Paris dress designs.

Flirt on, soft spinsters, flirt with time.
Order the crowded hours, vicariously tranced.
Know Africa and judge which prize-fighter was hurt,
How well the latest ballerina danced,
How cake, or love, was made. O flirt, my two aunts, flirt!

JOHN PUDNEY

Academic

How sad, they think, to see him homing nightly
In converse with himself across the quad,
Down by the river and the railway arch
To his gaunt villa and his bickering brood,
Their mother anchored by a hill of mending.
Such banal feelings—how they pity him.

By day his food is Plato, Machiavelli.
'Thought is a flower, gentlemen,' he says—
Tracing the thought in air until it grows
Like frost-flowers on the windows of the mind—
'Thought is a flower that has its roots in dung.'

What irony, they think, that one so nourished,
Perfect in all the classic commonwealths,
Himself so signally should lack the arts
To shine and burgeon in the College councils,
A worn-out battery, a nobody, a windbag.
'And yet,' they sigh, 'what has the old boy got,
That every time he talks he fills the hall?'

JAMES REEVES

Timothy Winters

Timothy Winters comes to school
With eyes as wide as a football-pool,
Ears like bombs and teeth like splinters:
A blitz of a boy is Timothy Winters.

His belly is white, his neck is dark,
And his hair is an exclamation-mark.
His clothes are enough to scare a crow
And through his britches the blue winds blow.

When teacher talks he won't hear a word
And he shoots down dead the arithmetic-bird,
He licks the patterns off his plate
And he's not even heard of the Welfare State.

Timothy Winters has bloody feet
And he lives in a house on Suez Street,
He sleeps in a sack on the kitchen floor
And they say there aren't boys like him any more.

Old Man Winters likes his beer
And his missus ran off with a bombardier,
Grandma sits in the grate with a gin
And Timothy's dosed with an aspirin.

The Welfare Worker lies awake
But the law's as tricky as a ten-foot snake,
So Timothy Winters drinks his cup
And slowly goes on growing up.

At Morning Prayers the Master helves
For children less fortunate than ourselves,
And the loudest response in the room is when
Timothy Winters roars 'Amen!'

So come one angel, come on ten:
Timothy Winters says 'Amen
Amen amen amen amen.'
Timothy Winters, Lord.
Amen.

CHARLES CAUSLEY

Epitaph

Mr. Heath-Stubbs as you must understand
Came of a gentleman's family out of Staffordshire
Of as good blood as any in England
But he was wall-eyed and his legs too spare.

His elbows and finger-joints could bend more ways than one
And in frosty weather would creak audibly
As to delight his friends he would give demonstration
Which he might have done in public for a small fee.

Amongst the more learned persons of his time
Having had his schooling in the University of Oxford
In Anglo-Saxon Latin ornithology and crime
Yet after four years he was finally not preferred.

Orthodox in beliefs as following the English Church
Barring some heresies he would have for recreation
Yet too often left these sound principles (as I am told) in the lurch
Being troubled with idleness, lechery, pride and dissipation.

In his youth he would compose poems in prose and verse
In a classical romantic manner which was pastoral
To which the best judges of the Age were not averse
And the public also but his profit was not financial.

Now having outlived his friends and most of his reputation
He is content to take his rest under these stones and grass
Not expecting but hoping that the Resurrection
Will not catch him unawares whenever it takes place.

JOHN HEATH-STUBBS

74

Incident on a Journey

One night I reached a cave: I slept, my head
Full of the air. There came about daybreak
A red-coat soldier to the mouth, who said
'I am not living, in hell's pains I ache,
    But I regret nothing.'

His forehead had a bloody wound whose streaming
The pallid staring face illuminated.
Whether his words were mine or his, in dreaming
I found they were my deepest thoughts translated.
    '*I regret nothing:*

'Turn your closed eyes to see upon these walls
A mural scratched there by an earlier man,
And coloured with the blood of animals:
Showing humanity beyond its span,
    Regretting nothing.

'No plausible nostalgia, no brown shame
I had when treating with my enemies.
And always when a living impulse came
I acted, and my action made me wise.
    And I regretted nothing.

'I as possessor of unnautural strength
Was hunted, one day netted in a brawl;
A minute far beyond a minute's length
Took from me passion, strength, and life, and all.
    But I regretted nothing.

'Their triumph left my body in the dust;
The dust and beer still clotting in my hair
When I rise lonely, will-less. Where I must
I go, and what I must I bear.
    And I regret nothing.

'My lust runs yet and is unsatisfied,
My hate throbs yet but I am feeble-limbed;
If as an animal I could have died
My death had scattered instinct to the wind,
    Regrets as nothing.'

Later I woke. I started to my feet.
The valley light, the mist already going.
I was alive and felt my body sweet,
Uncaked blood in all its channels flowing.
    I would regret nothing.

THOM GUNN

Jesus and His Mother

My only son, more God's than mine,
Stay in this garden ripe with pears.
The yielding of their substance wears
A modest and contented shine:
And when they weep with age, not brine
But lazy syrup are their tears.
'I am my own and not my own.'

He seemed much like another man,
That silent foreigner who trod
Outside my door with lily rod:
How could I know what I began
Meeting the eyes more furious than
The eyes of Joseph, those of God?
I was my own and not my own.

And who are these twelve labouring men?
I do not understand your words:
I taught you speech, we named the birds,
You marked their big migrations then
Like any child. So turn again
To silence from the place of crowds.
'I am my own and not my own.'

Why are you sullen when I speak?
Here are your tools, the saw and knife
And hammer on your bench. Your life
Is measured here in week and week
Planed as the furniture you make,
And I will teach you like a wife
To be my own and all my own.

Who like an arrogant wind blown
Where he may please, needs no content?
Yet I remember how you went
To speak with scholars in furred gown,
I hear an outcry in the town;
Who carried that dark instrument?
'One all his own and not his own.'

Treading the green and nimble sward
I stare at a strange shadow thrown.
Are you the boy I bore alone,
No doctor near to cut the cord?
I cannot reach to call you Lord,
Answer me as my only son.
'I am my own and not my own.'

THOM GUNN

78

An Arundel Tomb

Side by side, their faces blurred,
The earl and countess lie in stone,
Their proper habits vaguely shown
As jointed armour, stiffened pleat,
And that faint hint of the absurd—
The little dogs under their feet.

Such plainness of the pre-baroque
Hardly involves the eye, until
It meets his left-hand gauntlet, still
Clasped empty in the other; and
One sees, with a sharp tender shock,
His hand withdrawn, holding her hand.

They would not think to lie so long.
Such faithfulness in effigy
Was just a detail friends would see:
A sculptor's sweet commissioned grace
Thrown off in helping to prolong
The Latin names around the base.

They would not guess how early in
Their supine stationary voyage
The air would change to soundless damage,
Turn the old tenantry away;
How soon succeeding eyes begin
To look, not read. Rigidly they

Persisted, linked, through lengths and breadths
Of time. Snow fell, undated. Light
Each summer thronged the grass. A bright
Litter of birdcalls strewed the same
Bone-riddled ground. And up the paths
The endless altered people came,

Washing at their identity.
Now, helpless in the hollow of
An unarmorial age, a trough
Of smoke in slow suspended skeins
Above their scrap of history,
Only their attitude remains.

Time has transfigured them into
Untruth. The stone fidelity
They hardly meant has come to be
Their final blazon, and to prove
Our almost-instinct almost true:
What will survive of us is love.

PHILIP LARKIN

Wind

This house has been far out at sea all night,
The woods crashing through darkness, the booming hills,
Winds stampeding the fields under the window
Floundering black astride and blinding wet

Till day rose; then under an orange sky
The hills had new places, and wind wielded
Blade-like, luminous black and emerald,
Flexing like the lens of a mad eye.

At noon I scaled along the house-side as far as
The coal-house door. I dared once to look up—
Through the brunt wind that dented the balls of my eyes
The tent of the hills drummed and strained its guyrope,

The fields quivering, the skyline a grimace,
At any second to bang and vanish with a flap:
The wind flung a magpie away and a black-
Back gull bent like an iron bar slowly. The house

Rang like some fine green goblet in the note
That any second would shatter it. Now deep
In chairs, in front of the great fire, we grip
Our hearts and cannot entertain book, thought,

Or each other. We watch the fire blazing,
And feel the roots of the house move, but sit on,
Seeing the window tremble to come in,
Hearing the stones cry out under the horizons.

TED HUGHES

Pike

Pike, three inches long, perfect
Pike in all parts, green tigering the gold.
Killers from the egg: the malevolent aged grin.
They dance on the surface among the flies.

Or move, stunned by their own grandeur,
Over a bed of emerald, silhouette
Of submarine delicacy and horror,
A hundred feet long in their world.

In ponds, under the heat-struck lily pads—
Gloom of their stillness:
Logged on last year's black leaves, watching
    upwards.
Or hung in an amber cavern of weeds.

The jaws' hooked clamp and fangs
Not to be changed at this date;
A life subdued to its instrument;
The gills kneading quietly, and the pectorals.

Three we kept behind glass,
Jungled in weed: three inches, four,
And four and a half: fed fry to them—
Suddenly there were two. Finally one

With a sag belly and the grin it was born with.
And indeed they spare nobody.
Two, six pounds each, over two feet long,
High and dry and dead in the willow-herb—

One jammed past its gills down the other's gullet:
The outside eye stared: as a vice locks—
The same iron in this eye
Though its film shrank in death.

The pond I fished, fifty yards across,
Whose lilies and muscular tench
Had outlasted every visible stone
Of the monastery that planted them—

Stilled legendary depth:
It was as deep as England. It held
Pike too immense to stir, so immense and old
That past nightfall I dared not cast

But silently cast and fished
With the hair frozen on my head
For what might move, for what eye might move.
The still splashes on the dark pond,

Owls hushing the floating woods
Frail on my ear against the dream
Darkness beneath night's darkness had freed,
That rose slowly towards me, watching.

TED HUGHES

Hawk Roosting

I sit in the top of the wood, my eyes closed.
Inaction, no falsifying dream
Between my hooked head and hooked feet:
Or in sleep rehearse perfect kills and eat.

The convenience of the high trees!
The air's buoyancy and the sun's ray
Are of advantage to me;
And the earth's face upward for my inspection.

My feet are locked upon the rough bark.
It took the whole of Creation
To produce my foot, my each feather:
Now I hold Creation in my foot

Or fly up, and revolve it all slowly—
I kill where I please because it is all mine.
There is no sophistry in my body:
My manners are tearing off heads—

The allotment of death.
For the one path of my flight is direct
Through the bones of the living.
No arguments assert my right:

The sun is behind me.
Nothing has changed since I began.
My eye has permitted no change.
I am going to keep things like this.

TED HUGHES

84

The Lonely Man

A cat sits on the pavement by the house.
It lets itself be touched, then slides away.
A girl goes by in a hood; the winter noon's
Long shadows lengthen. The cat is gray,
It sits there. It sits there all day, every day.

A collie bounds into my arms: he is a dog
And, therefore, finds nothing human alien.
He lives at the preacher's with a pair of cats
The soft half-Persian sidles to me;
Indoors, the old white one watches blindly.

How cold it is! Some snow slides from a roof
When a squirrel jumps off it to a squirrel-proof
Feeding-station; and, a lot and two yards down,
A fat spaniel snuffles out to me
And sobers me with his untrusting frown.

He worries about his yard: past it, it's my affair
If I halt Earth in her track—his duty's done.
And the cat and the collie worry about the old one:
They come, when she's out too, so uncertainly . . . .
It's my block; I know them, just as they know me.

As for the others, those who wake up every day
And feed these, keep the houses, ride away
To work—I don't know them, they don't know me.
Are we friends or enemies? Why, who can say?
We nod to each other sometimes, in humanity,

Or search one another's faces with a yearning
Remnant of faith that's almost animal . . . .
The gray cat that just sits there: surely it is learning
To be a man; will find, soon, *some especial*
Opening in a good firm for a former cat.

RANDALL JARRELL

Dunbarton

When Uncle Devereux died,
Daddy was still on sea-duty in the Pacific,
it seemed spontaneous and proper
for Mr. MacDonald, the farmer,
Karl, the chauffeur, and even my Grandmother
to say, 'your Father.' They meant my Grandfather.

He was my Father. I was his son.
On our yearly autumn get-aways from Boston
to the family graveyard in Dunbarton,
he took the wheel himself—
like an admiral at the helm.
Freed from Karl and chuckling over the gas he was saving,
he let his motor roller-coaster
out of control down each hill.
We stopped at the *Priscilla* in Nashua
for brownies and root-beer,
and later 'pumped ship' together in the Indian Summer . . . .

At the graveyard, a suave Venetian Christ
gave a sheepdog's nursing patience
to Grandfather's Aunt Lottie,
his Mother, the stone but not the bones
of his Father, Francis.
Failing as when Francis Winslow could count
them on his fingers,
the clump of virgin pine still stretched patchy ostrich necks
over the disused millpond's fragrantly woodstained water,
a reddish blur,
like the ever-blackening wine-dark coat
in our portrait of Edward Winslow
once sheriff for George the Second,
the sire of bankrupt Tories.

Grandfather and I
raked leaves from our dead forbears,
defied the dank weather
with 'dragon' bonfires.
Our helper, Mr. Burroughs,
had stood with Sherman at Shiloh—
his thermos of shockless coffee
was milk and grounds,
his illegal home-made claret
was as sugary as grape jelly
in a tumbler capped with paraffin.

I borrowed Grandfather's cane
carved with the names and altitudes
of Norwegian mountains he had scaled—
more a weapon than a crutch.
I lanced it in the fauve ooze for newts.
In a tobacco tin after capture, the umber yellow mature newts
lost their leopard spots,
lay grounded as numb
as scrolls of candied grapefruit peel.
I saw myself as a young newt,
neurasthenic, scarlet
and wild in the wild coffee-coloured water.

In the mornings I cuddled like a paramour
in my Grandfather's bed,
while he scouted about the chattering greenwood stove.
My Grandfather found
his grandchild's fogbound solitudes
sweeter than human society.

ROBERT LOWELL

88

The Slow Starter

A watched clock never moves, they said:
Leave it alone and you'll grow up.
Nor will the sulking holiday train
Start sooner if you stamp your feet.
  He left the clock to go its way;
  The whistle blew, the train went gay.

Do not press me so, she said;
Leave me alone and I will write
But not just yet, I am sure you know
The problem. Do not count the days.
  He left the calendar alone;
  The postman knocked, no letter came.

O never force the pace, they said;
Leave it alone, you have lots of time,
Your kind of work is none the worse
For slow maturing. Do not rush.
  He took their tip, he took his time,
  And found his time and talent gone.

Oh you have had your chance, It said;
Left it alone and it was one.
Who said a watched clock never moves?
Look at it now. Your chance was I.
  He turned and saw the accusing clock
  Race like a torrent round a rock.

LOUIS MACNEICE

The Goodnight

He stood still by her bed
Watching his daughter breathe,
The dark and silver head,
The fingers curled beneath,
And thought : Though she may have
Intelligence and charm
And luck, they will not save
Her life from every harm.

The lives of children are
Dangerous to their parents
With fire, water, air,
And other accidents;
And some, for a child's sake,
Anticipating doom,
Empty the world to make
The world safe as a room.

Who could endure the pain
That was Laocoön's?
Twisting, he saw again
In the same coil his sons.
Plumed in his father's skill,
Young Icarus flew higher
Toward the sun, until
He fell in rings of fire.

A man who cannot stand
Children's perilous play,
With lifted voice and hand
Drives the children away.
Out of sight, out of reach,
The tumbling children pass;
He sits on an empty beach,
Holding an empty glass.

Who said that tenderness
Will turn the heart to stone?
May I endure her weakness
As I endure my own.
Better to say goodnight
To breathing flesh and blood
Each night as though the night
Were always only good.

LOUIS SIMPSON

First, Goodbye

First, you will say goodbye. You will turn
    And for what you think is the last time gaze from the window
    To the bright and battering street headlong below.
Behind your eyes, your smile, the tears will burn.

You will not let them fall. You will stand
    As if you were a child or a cripple unable to walk.
    You will try though the words are like glass, you will try to talk,
But you will manage only a pathetic gesture of the hand.

All this is ordinary. You will be aware
    Of my presence behind you the world of our words away.
    And you will know, you will know there is nothing that I can say;
And then you will hear with your heart the dumbness of my despair

Articulate in the silence; it will cry
    Out in such a remonstrance of love that you will know
    No window or door or street may let you go,
Or your lips or my lips utter a last goodbye.

JOHN SMITH

92

One Flesh

Lying apart now, each in a separate bed,
He with a book, keeping the light on late,
She like a girl dreaming of childhood,
All men elsewhere—it is as if they wait
Some new event: the book he holds unread,
Her eyes fixed on the shadows overhead.

Tossed up like flotsam from a former passion,
How cool they lie. They hardly ever touch,
Or if they do it is like a confession
Of having little feeling—or too much.
Chastity faces them, a destination
For which their whole lives were a preparation.

Strangely apart, yet strangely close together,
Silence between them like a thread to hold
And not wind in. And time itself's a feather
Touching them gently. Do they know they're old,
These two who are my father and my mother
Whose fire from which I came, has now grown cold?

ELIZABETH JENNINGS

By Ferry to the Island

We crossed by ferry to the bare island
where sheep and cows stared coldly through the wind—
the sea behind us with its silver water,
the silent ferryman standing in the stern
clutching his coat about him like old iron.

We landed from the ferry and went inland
past a small church down to the winding shore
where a white seagull fallen from the failing
chill and ancient daylight lay so pure
and softly breasted that it made more dear

the lesser white around us. There we sat
sheltered by a rock beside the sea.
Someone made coffee, someone played the fool
in a high rising voice for two hours.
The sea's language was more grave and harsh.

And one sat there whose dress was white and cool.
The fool sparkled his wit that she might hear
new diamonds turning on her naked finger.
What might the sea think or the dull sheep
lifting its head through heavy Sunday sleep?

And later, going home, a moon rising
at the end of a cart-track, minimum of red,
the wind being dark, imperfect cows staring
out of their half-intelligence, and a plough
lying on its side in the cold, raw

naked twilight, there began to move
slowly, like heavy water, in the heart
the image of the gull and of that dress,
both being white and out of the darkness rising
the moon ahead of us with its rusty ring.

IAIN CRICHTON SMITH

The Moon
and the Yew Tree

This is the light of the mind, cold and planetary.
The trees of the mind are black. The light is blue.
The grasses unload their griefs on my feet as if I
    were God,
Prickling my ankles and murmuring of their humility.
Fumey, spiritous mists inhabit this place
Separated from my house by a row of headstones.
I simply cannot see where there is to get to.

The moon is no door. It is a face in its own right,
White as a knuckle and terribly upset.
It drags the sea after it like a dark crime; it is quiet
With the O-gape of complete despair. I live here.
Twice on Sunday, the bells startle the sky—
Eight great tongues affirming the Resurrection.
At the end, they soberly bong out their names.

The yew tree points up. It has a Gothic shape.
The eyes lift after it and find the moon.
The moon is my mother. She is not sweet like Mary.
Her blue garments unloose small bats and owls.
How I would like to believe in tenderness—
The face of the effigy, gentled by candles,
Bending, on me in particular, its mild eyes.

I have fallen a long way. Clouds are flowering
Blue and mystical over the face of the stars.
Inside the church, the saints will be all blue,
Floating on their delicate feet over the cold pews,
Their hands and faces stiff with holiness.
The moon sees nothing of this. She is bald and wild.
And the message of the yew tree is blackness—
    blackness and silence.

SYLVIA PLATH

96

Balloons

Since Christmas they have lived with us,
Guileless and clear,
Oval soul-animals,
Taking up half the space,
Moving and rubbing on the silk

Invisible air drifts,
Giving a shriek and pop
When attacked, then scooting to rest, barely trembling.
Yellow cathead, blue fish—
Such queer moons we live with

Instead of dead furniture!
Straw mats, white walls
And these travelling
Globes of thin air, red, green,
Delighting

The heart like wishes or free
Peacocks blessing
Old ground with a feather
Beaten in starry metals.
Your small

Brother is making
His balloon squeak like a cat.
Seeming to see
A funny pink world he might eat on the other side of it,
He bites,

Then sits
Back, fat jug
Contemplating a world clear as water,
A red
Shred in his little fist.

SYLVIA PLATH

Blackberrying

Nobody in the lane, and nothing, nothing but blackberries,
Blackberries on either side, though on the right mainly,
A blackberry alley, going down in hooks, and a sea
Somewhere at the end of it, heaving. Blackberries
Big as the ball of my thumb, and dumb as eyes
Ebon in the hedges, fat
With blue-red juices. These they squander on my fingers.
I had not asked for such a blood sisterhood; they must love
                                                                    me.
They accommodate themselves to my milkbottle, flattening
                                                          their sides.

Overhead go the choughs in black, cacophonous flocks—
Bits of burnt paper wheeling in a blown sky.
Theirs is the only voice, protesting, protesting.
I do not think the sea will appear at all.
The high, green meadows are glowing, as if lit from within.
I come to one bush of berries so ripe it is a bush of flies,
Hanging their bluegreen bellies and their wing panes in a
                                                    Chinese screen.
The honey-feast of the berries has stunned them; they believe
                                                          in heaven.
One more hook, and the berries and bushes end.

The only thing to come now is the sea.
From between two hills a sudden wind funnels at me,
Slapping its phantom laundry in my face.
These hills are too green and sweet to have tasted salt.
I follow the sheep path between them. A last hook brings me
To the hills' northern face, and the face is orange rock
That looks out on nothing, nothing but a great space
Of white and pewter lights, and a din like silversmiths
Beating and beating at an intractable metal.

SYLVIA PLATH

The Lesson

'Your father's gone,' my bald headmaster said.
His shiny dome and brown tobacco jar
Splintered at once in tears. It wasn't grief.
I cried for knowledge which was bitterer
Than any grief. For there and then I knew
That grief has uses—that a father dead
Could bind the bully's fist a week or two;
And then I cried for shame, then for relief.

I was a month past ten when I learnt this:
I still remember how the noise was stilled
In school-assembly when my grief came in.
Some goldfish in a bowl quietly sculled
Around their shining prison on its shelf.
They were indifferent. All the other eyes
Were turned towards me. Somewhere in myself
Pride, like a goldfish, flashed a sudden fin.

EDWARD LUCIE-SMITH

Young

A thousand doors ago
when I was a lonely kid
in a big house with four
garages and it was summer
as long as I could remember,
I lay on the lawn at night,
clover wrinkling under me,
the wise stars bedding over me,
my mother's window a funnel
of yellow heat running out,
my father's window, half shut,
an eye where sleepers pass,
and the boards of the house
were smooth and white as wax
and probably a million leaves
sailed on their strange stalks
as the crickets ticked together
and I, in my brand new body,
which was not a woman's yet,
told the stars my questions
and thought God could really see
the heat and the painted light,
elbows, knees, dreams, goodnight.

ANNE SEXTON

Elegy for Alfred Hubbard

Hubbard is dead, the old plumber;
who will mend our burst pipes now,
the tap that has dripped all the summer,
testing the sink's overflow?

No other like him. Young men with knowledge
of new techniques, theories from books,
may better his work straight from college,
but who will challenge his squint-eyed looks

in kitchen, bathroom, under floorboards,
rules of thumb which were often wrong;
seek as erringly stopcocks in cupboards,
or make a job last half as long?

He was a man who knew the ginnels,
alleyways, streets,—the whole district;
family secrets, minor annals,
time-honoured fictions fused to fact.

Seventy years of gossip muttered
under his cap, his tufty thatch,
so that his talk was slow and clotted,
hard to follow, and too much.

As though nothing fell, none vanished,
and time were the maze of Cheetham Hill,
in which the dead,—with jobs unfinished—,
waited to hear him ring the bell.

For much he never got round to doing,
but meant to, when the weather bucked up,
or worsened, or when his pipe was drawing,
or when he'd finished this cup.

I thought time, he forgot so often,
had forgotten him, but here's Death's pomp
over his house, and by the coffin
the son who will inherit his blowlamp,

tools, workshop, cart, and cornet,
(pride of Cheetham Prize Brass Band),—
and there's his mourning widow, Janet,
stood at the gate he'd promised to mend.

Soon he will make his final journey;
shaved and silent, strangely trim,
with never a pause to talk to anybody: how arrow-like, for him!

In St Mark's Church,—whose dismal tower
he pointed and painted when a lad—,
they will sing his praises amidst flowers,
while, somewhere, a cellar starts to flood,

and the housewife banging his front-door knocker
is not surprised to find him gone,
and runs for Thwaite, who's a better worker,
and sticks at a job until it's done.

TONY CONNOR

A Christmas Hymn

*And some of the Pharisees from among the multitude said
unto him, Master, rebuke thy disciples.
And he answered and said unto them, I tell you that, if these
should hold their peace, the stones would immediately cry out.*

ST LUKE XIX,   39–40

A stable-lamp is lighted
Whose glow shall wake the sky;
The stars shall bend their voices,
And every stone shall cry.
And every stone shall cry,
And straw like gold shall shine;
A barn shall harbour heaven,
A stall become a shrine.

This child through David's city
Shall ride in triumph by;
The palm shall strew its branches,
And every stone shall cry.
And every stone shall cry,
Though heavy, dull, and dumb,
And lie within the roadway
To pave his kingdom come.

Yet he shall be forsaken,
And yielded up to die;
The sky shall groan and darken,
And every stone shall cry.
And every stone shall cry
For stony hearts of men:
God's blood upon the spearhead,
God's love refused again.

But now, as at the ending,
The low is lifted high;
The stars shall bend their voices,
And every stone shall cry.
And every stone shall cry
In praises of the child
By whose descent among us
The worlds are reconciled.

RICHARD WILBUR

Innocent's Song

Who's that knocking on the window,
Who's that standing at the door,
What are all those presents
Lying on the kitchen floor?

Who is the smiling stranger
With hair as white as gin,
What is he doing with the children
And who could have let him in?

Why has he rubies on his fingers,
A cold, cold crown on his head,
Why, when he caws his carol,
Does the salty snow run red?

Why does he ferry my fireside
As a spider on a thread,
His fingers made of fuses
And his tongue of gingerbread?

Why does the world before him
Melt in a million suns,
Why do his yellow, yearning eyes
Burn like saffron buns?

Watch where he comes walking
Out of the Christmas flame,
Dancing, double-talking:

Herod is his name.

CHARLES CAUSLEY

The Ballad of Mrs. Noah

Mrs Noah in the Ark
wove a great nightgown out of the dark,
did Mrs Noah,

had her own hearth in the Holy Boat,
two cats, two books, two cooking pots,
had Mrs Noah,

two pints of porter, two pecks of peas,
and a stir in her stew of memories.

Oh, that was a town, said Mrs Noah,
that the Lord in His wrath
did up and drown!

I liked its windows and I liked its trees.
Save me a little, Lord, I prayd on my knees.
And now, Lord save me, I've two of each!
apple, apricot, cherry and peach.

How shall I manage it? I've two of them all—
hairy, scaly, leathery, slick,
fluttery, buttery, thin and thick,
shaped like a stick, shaped like a ball,
too tiny to see, and much too tall.

I've all that I askd for and more and more,
windows and chimneys, and a great store
of needles and pins, of outs and ins,
and a regular forgive-us for some of my sins.

    She wove a great nightgown out of the dark
    decorated like a Sunday Park
    with clouds of black thread to remember her grief
    sewn about with bright flowers to give relief,

and, in a grim humor, a border all round
with the little white bones of the wicked drownd.

Tell me, Brother, what do you see?
said Mrs Noah to the Lowly Worm.

O Mother, the Earth is black, black.
To my crawlly bride and lowly me
the Earth is bitter as can be
where the Dead lie down and never come back,
said the blind Worm.

Tell me, Brother, what do *you* see?
said Mrs Noah to the sleeping Cat.

O Mother, the weather is dreadful wet.
I'll keep house for you wherever you'll be.
I'll sit by the fireside and be your pet.
And as long as I'm dry I'll purr for free,
said snug-loving Cat.

Tell me, Brother, has the Flood gone?
said Mrs Noah to the searching Crow.

No. No. No home in sight.
I fly thru the frightful waste alone,
said the carrion Crow.
The World is an everlasting Night.

Now that can't be true, Noah, Old Noah,
said the good Housewife to her good Spouse.
How long must we go in this floating House?
growing old and hope cold,
Husband, without new land?

And then Glory-Be with a Rainbow to-boot!
the Dove returnd with an Olive Shoot.

Tell me, Brother, what have we here,
my Love? to the Dove said Mrs Noah.

It's a Branch of All-Cheer
you may wear on your nightgown all the long year
as a boa, Mrs Noah, said the Dove,
with God's Love!

Then out from the Ark
in her nightgown all dark
with only her smile to betoken the Day
and a wreath-round of olive leaves

Mrs Noah steppd down
into the same old wicked repenting
Lord-Will-We-Ever recently recoverd
comfortable World-Town.

O where have you been, Mother Noah, Mother Noah?

I've had a great Promise for only Tomorrow.
In the Ark of Sleep I've been on a sail
over the wastes of the world's sorrow.

And the Promise? the Tomorrow? Mother Noah, Mother Noah?

Ah! the Rainbow's awake
and we will not fail!

ROBERT DUNCAN

108

The Rabbit

We are going to see the rabbit.
We are going to see the rabbit.
Which rabbit, people say?
Which rabbit, ask the children?
Which rabbit?
The only rabbit,
The only rabbit in England,
Sitting behind a barbed-wire fence
Under the floodlights, neon lights,
Sodium lights,
Nibbling grass
On the only patch of grass
In England, in England
(Except the grass by the hoardings
Which doesn't count.)
We are going to see the rabbit
And we must be there on time.

First we shall go by escalator,
Then we shall go by underground,
And then we shall go by motorway
And then by helicopterway,
And the last ten yards we shall have to go
On foot.

And now we are going
All the way to see the rabbit,
We are nearly there,
We are longing to see it,
And so is the crowd
Which is here in thousands
With mounted policemen
And big loudspeakers
And bands and banners,
And everyone has come a long way.
But soon we shall see it
Sitting and nibbling
The blades of grass
On the only patch of grass
In—but something has gone wrong!
Why is everyone so angry,
Why is everyone jostling
And slanging and complaining?

The rabbit has gone,
Yes, the rabbit has gone.
He has actually burrowed down into the earth
And made himself a warren, under the earth,
Despite all these people.
And what shall we do?
What *can* we do?

It is all a pity, you must be disappointed,
Go home and do something else for today,
Go home again, go home for today.
For you cannot hear the rabbit, under the earth,
Remarking rather sadly to himself, by himself,
As he rests in his warren, under the earth:
'It won't be long, they are bound to come,
They are bound to come and find me, even here.'

ALAN BROWNJOHN

110

My Grandmother

She kept an antique shop—or it kept her.
Among Apostle spoons and Bristol glass,
The faded silks, the heavy furniture,
She watched her own reflection in the brass
Salvers and silver bowls, as if to prove
Polish was all, there was no need of love.

And I remember how I once refused
To go out with her, since I was afraid.
It was perhaps a wish not to be used
Like antique objects. Though she never said
That she was hurt, I still could feel the guilt
Of that refusal, guessing how she felt.

Later, too frail to keep a shop, she put
All her best things in one long narrow room,
The place smelt old, of things too long kept shut,
The smell of absences where shadows come
That can't be polished. There was nothing then
To give her own reflection back again.

And when she died I felt no grief at all,
Only the guilt of what I once refused.
I walked into her room among the tall
Sideboards and cupboards—things she never used
But needed; and no finger-marks were there,
Only the new dust falling through the air.

ELIZABETH JENNINGS

The Quagga

By mid-century there were two quaggas left,
And one of the two was male.
The cares of office weighed heavily on him.
When you are the only male of a species,
It is not easy to lead a normal sort of life.

The goats nibbled and belched in casual content;
They charged and skidded up and down their concrete
      mountain.
One might cut his throat on broken glass,
Another stray too near the tigers.
But they were zealous husbands; and the enclosure
      was always full,
Its rank air throbbing with ingenuous voices.

The quagga, however, was a man of destiny.
His wife, whom he had met rather late in her life,
Preferred to sleep, or complain of the food and
      the weather.
For their little garden was less than paradisiac,
With its artificial sun that either scorched or left
      you cold,
And savants with cameras eternally hanging around,
To perpetuate the only male quagga in the world.

Perhaps that was why he failed to do it himself.
It is all very well for goats and monkeys—
But the last male of a species is subject to peculiar
      pressures.
If ancient Satan had come slithering in, perhaps . . .
But instead the savants, with cameras and notebooks,
Writing sad stories of the decadence of quaggas.

And then one sultry afternoon he started raising Cain.
This angry young quagga kicked the bars and broke a
          camera;
He even tried to bite his astonished keeper.
He protested loud and clear against this and that,
Till the other animals became quite embarrassed
For he seemed to be calling them names.

Then he noticed his wife, awake with the noise,
And a curious feeling quivered round his belly.
He was Adam: there was Eve.
Galloping over to her, his head flung back,
He stumbled, and broke a leg, and had to be shot.

D. J. ENRIGHT

Circus Lion

Lumbering haunches, pussyfoot tread, a pride of
Lions under the arcs
Walk in, leap up, sit pedestalled there and glum
As a row of Dickensian clerks.

Their eyes are slag. Only a muscle flickering,
A bored, theatrical roar
Witness now to the furnaces that drove them
Exultant along the spoor.

In preyward, elastic leap they are sent through paper
Hoops at another's will
And a whip's crack: afterwards, in their cages,
They tear the provided kill.

Caught young, can this public animal ever dream of
Stars, distances and thunders?
Does he twitch in sleep for ticks, dried water-holes,
Rogue elephants, or hunters?

Sawdust, not burning desert, is the ground
Of his to-fro, to-fro pacing,
Barred with the zebra shadows that imply
Sun's free wheel, man's coercing.

See this abdicated beast, once king
Of them all, nibble his claws:
Not anger enough left—no, nor despair—
To break his teeth on the bars.

C. DAY LEWIS

The Starling

The starling is my darling, although
I don't much approve of its
Habits. Proletarian bird,
Nesting in holes and corners, making a mess,
And sometimes dropping its eggs
Just any old where—on the front lawn, for instance.

It thinks it can sing too. In springtime
They are on every rooftop, or high bough,
Or telegraph pole, blithering away
Discords, with clichés picked up
From the other melodists.

But go to Trafalgar Square,
And stand, about sundown, on the steps of St Martin's;
Mark then in the air,
The starlings, before they roost, at their evolutions—
Scores of starlings, wheeling,
Streaming and twisting, the whole murmuration
Turning like one bird: an image
Realized, of the City.

JOHN HEATH-STUBBS

Song of the Battery Hen

We can't grumble about accommodation:
we have a new concrete floor that's
always dry, four walls that are
painted white, and a sheet-iron roof
the rain drums on. A fan blows warm air
beneath our feet to disperse the smell
of chicken-shit and, on dull days,
fluorescent lighting sees us.

You can tell me: if you come by
the North door, I am in the twelfth pen
on the left-hand side of the third row
from the floor; and in that pen
I am usually the middle one of three.
But, even without directions, you'd
discover me. I have the same orange-
red comb, yellow beak and auburn
feathers, but as the door opens and you
hear above the electric fan a kind of
one-word wail, I am the one
who sounds loudest in my head.

Listen. Outside this house there's an
orchard with small moss-green apple
trees; beyond that, two fields of
cabbages; then, on the far side of
the road, a broiler house. Listen:
one cockerel grows out of there, as
tall and proud as the first hour of sun.
Sometimes I stop calling with the others
to listen, and wonder if he hears me.

The next time you come here, look for me.
Notice the way I sound inside my head.
God made us all quite differently,
and blessed us with this expensive home.

EDWIN BROCK

Grace to be said at the Supermarket

That God of ours, the Great Geometer,
Does something for us here, where He hath put
(if you want to put it that way) things in shape,
Compressing the little lambs in orderly cubes,
Making the roast a decent cylinder,
Fairing the tin ellipsoid of a ham,
Getting the luncheon meat anonymous
In squares and oblongs with the edges bevelled
Or rounded (streamlined, maybe, for greater speed).

Praise Him, He hath conferred aesthetic distance
Upon our appetites, and on the bloody
Mess of our birthright, our unseemly need,
Imposed significant form. Through Him the brutes
Enter the pure Euclidean kingdom of number,
Free of their bulging and blood-swollen lives
They come to us holy, in cellophane
Transparencies, in the mystical body,

That we may look unflinchingly on death
As the greatest good, like a philosopher should.

HOWARD NEMEROV

Tea in a Space-Ship

In this world a tablecloth need not be laid
On any table, but is spread out anywhere
Upon the always equidistant and
Invisible legs of gravity's wild air.

The tea, which never would grow cold,
Gathers itself into a wet and steaming ball,
And hurls its liquid molecules at anybody's head,
Or dances, eternal bilboquet,
In and out of the suspended cups up-
Ended in the weightless hands
Of chronically nervous jerks
Who yet would never spill a drop,
Their mouths agape for passing cakes.

Lumps of sparkling sugar
Sling themselves out of their crystal bowl
With a disordered fountain's
Ornamental stops and starts.
The milk describes a permanent parabola
Girdled with satellites of spinning tarts.

The future lives with graciousness.
The hostess finds her problems eased,
For there is honey still for tea
And butter keeps the ceiling greased.

She will provide, of course,
No cake-forks, spoons or knives.
They are so sharp, so dangerously gadabout,
It is regarded as a social misdemeanour
To put them out.

JAMES KIRKUP

119

Love in a Space-Suit

Dear, when on some distant planet
We, love's protestants, alight,
How, in our deep-space-diver suits
Shall our devoted limbs unite?

You shall have those ruby lips
In a helmet-bowl, inverted
On your golden locks, enclosed:
Your starry eyes shall be inserted
In a plastic contact-vizor
To keep out the stellar cold.
And your teeth of pearls shall chatter
On a tongue too hot to hold.

Dear, those pretty little fingers
Shall be cased with lead around,
And your snowy breasts, my dove,
With insulating-tape be bound.
There your lovely legs, my sweet
In asbestos boots shall stump;
And a grim all-metal corset
Shall depress that witty rump.

How shall I, in suits of iron
Or of aluminium
Communicate my body's fire
In love's planetarium?
Darling, must we kiss by knocking
Bowl on bowl, a glassy bliss?
Must we lie apart for aye,
Not far, but not as near as this?

Nay! before I will renounce
My lust for earth and love of you,
I shall have us both, dear, fitted
With a space-suit made for two.

JAMES KIRKUP

Life Cycle
of Common Man

Roughly figured, this man of moderate habits,
This average consumer of the middle class,
Consumed in the course of his average life span
Just under half a million cigarettes,
Four thousand fifths of gin and about
A quarter as much vermouth; he drank
Maybe a hundred thousand cups of coffee,
And counting his parents' share it cost
Something like half a million dollars
To put him through life. How many beasts
Died to provide him with meat, belt and shoes
Cannot be certainly said.
                              But anyhow,
It is in this way that a man travels through time,
Leaving behind him a lengthening trail
Of empty bottles and bones, of broken shoes,
Frayed collars and worn out or outgrown
Diapers and dinnerjackets, silk ties and slickers.

Given the energy and security thus achieved,
He did . . .? What? The usual things, of course,
The eating, dreaming, drinking and begetting,
And he worked for the money which was to pay
For the eating, et cetera, which were necessary
If he were to go on working for the money, et cetera,
But chiefly he talked. As the bottles and bones
Accumulated behind him, the words proceeded
Steadily from the front of his face as he
Advanced into the silence and made it verbal.
Who can tally the tale of his words? A lifetime
Would barely suffice for their repetition;
If you merely printed all his commas the result
Would be a very large volume, and the number of times

He said 'thank you' or 'very little sugar, please,'
Would stagger the imagination. There were also
Witticisms, platitudes, and statements beginning
'It seems to me' or 'As I always say'.

Consider the courage in all that, and behold the man
Walking into deep silence, with the ectoplastic
Cartoon's balloon of speech proceeding
Steadily out of the front of his face, the words
Borne along on the breath which is his spirit
Telling the numberless tale of his untold Word
Which makes the world his apple, and forces him to eat.

HOWARD NEMEROV

122

Dreaming in the Shanghai Restaurant

I would like to be that elderly Chinese gentleman.
He wears a gold watch with a gold bracelet,
But a shirt without sleeves or tie.
He has good luck moles on his face, but is not
    disfigured with fortune.
His wife resembles him, but is still a handsome woman,
She has never bound her feet or her belly.
Some of the party are his children, it seems,
And some his grandchildren;
No generation appears to intimidate another.
He is interested in people, without wanting to
    convert them or pervert them.
He eats with gusto, but not with lust;
And he drinks, but is not drunk.
He is content with his age, which has always suited him.
When he discusses a dish with the pretty waitress,
It is the dish he discusses, not the waitress.
The table-cloth is not so clean as to show indifference,
Not so dirty as to signify a lack of manners.
He proposes to pay the bill but knows he will not be
    allowed to.
He walks to the door like a man who doesn't fret
    about being respected, since he is;
A daughter or granddaughter opens the door for him,
And he thanks her.
It has been a satisfying evening. Tomorrow
Will be a satisfying morning. In between
    he will sleep satisfactorily.
I guess that for him it is peace in his time.
It would be agreeable to be this Chinese gentleman.

D. J. ENRIGHT

123

This Landscape, These People

I

My eighth spring in England I walk among
The silver birches of Putney Heath,
Stepping over twigs and stones: being stranger,
I see but do not touch: only the earth
Permits an attachment. I do not wish
To be seen, and move, eyes at my sides, like a fish.

And do they notice me, I wonder, these
Englishmen strolling with stiff country strides?
I lean against a tree, my eyes are knots
In its bark, my skin the wrinkles in its sides.
I leap hedges, duck under chestnut boughs,
And through the black clay let my swift heels trail like ploughs.

A child at a museum, England for me
Is an exhibit within a glass case.
The country, like an antique chair, has a rope
Across it. I may not sit, only pace
Its frontiers. I slip through ponds, jump ditches,
Through galleries of ferns see England in pictures.

II

My seventeen years in India, I swam
Along the silver beaches of Bombay,
Pulled coconuts from the sky and tramped
Red horizons with the swagger and sway
Of Romantic youth; with the impudence
Of a native tongue, I cried for independence.

A troupe came to town, marched through villages;
  Began with two tight-rope walkers, eyes gay
  And bamboos and rope on their bare shoulders;
  A snake-charmer joined them, beard long and grey,
  Baskets of cobras on his turbaned head;
Through villages marched: children, beating on drums, led

Them from village to village, and jugglers
  Joined them and swallowers of swords, eaters
  Of fire brandishing flames through the thick air,
  Jesters with tongues obscene as crows', creatures
  Of the earth: stray dogs, lean jackals, a cow;
Stamping, shouting, entertaining, making a row

From village to village they marched to town;
  Conjurors to bake bread out of earth, poets
  To recite epics at night. The troupe, grown
  Into a nation, halted, squirmed: the sets
  For its act, though improvised, were re-cast
From the frames of an antique, slow-moving, dead past.

India halted: as suddenly as a dog,
  Barking, hangs out his tongue, stifles his cry.
  An epic turned into a monologue
  Of death. The rope lay stiff across the country;
  All fires were eaten, swallowed all the swords;
The horizons paled, then thickened, blackened with crows.

Born to this continent, all was mine
  To pluck and taste: pomegranates to purple
  My tongue and chillies to burn my mouth. Stones
  Were there to kick. This landscape, these people—
  Bound by the rope and consumed by their own fire.
Born here, among these people, I was a stranger.

III

This landscape, these people! Silver birches
  With polished trunks chalked around a chestnut.
  All is fall-of-night still. No thrush reaches
  Into the earth for worms, nor pulls at the root
  Of a crocus. Dogs have led their masters home.
I stroll, head bowed, hearing only the sound of loam

At my heel's touch. Now I am intimate
  With England; we meet, secret as lovers.
  I pluck leaves and speak into the air's mouth;
  As a woman's hair, I deck with flowers
  The willow's branches; I sit by the pond,
My eyes are stars in its stillness; as with a wand,

I stir the water with a finger until
  It tosses waves, until countries appear
  From its dark bed: the road from Putney Hill
  Runs across oceans into the harbour
  Of Bombay. To this country I have come.
Stranger or an inhabitant, this is my home.

ZULFIKAR GHOSE

Autobiographical Note

Beeston, the place, near Nottingham:
We lived there for three years or so.
Each Saturday at two-o'clock
We queued up for the matinée,
All the kids for streets around
With snotty noses, giant caps,
Cut down coats and heavy boots,
The natural enemies of cops
And schoolteachers. Profane and hoarse
We scrambled, yelled and fought until
The Picture Palace opened up
And we, like Hamelin children, forced
Our bony way into the hall.
That much is easy to recall;
Also the reek of chewing-gum,
Gob-stoppers and liquorice,
But of the flickering myths themselves
Not much remains. The hero was
A milky wide-brimmed hat, a shape
Astride the arched white stallion;
The villain's horse and hat were black.
Disbelief did not exist
And laundered virtue always won
With quicker gun and harder fist,
And all of us applauded it.
Yet I remember moments when
In solitude I'd find myself
Brooding on the sooty man,
The bristling villain, who could move
Imagination in a way
The well-shaved hero never could,
And even warm the nervous heart
With something oddly close to love.

VERNON SCANNELL

The 'Dorset Nose'

Startling to observe on the face of a Dorset yeoman,
Over his darts and beer,
The powerful nose of a grave and ancient Roman,
Imperious, austere.

Yet each generation, weaving in its buried Romes
An endless cycle of return,
Unearths among its normal chromosomes
This unexpected urn;

For Caesar's legions, claiming our land as his
When they had quelled the Gauls,
Did not employ their whole four centuries
Marching and building walls.

Though scorning their master's treatise on defence,
His interest in Latin prose,
They shared his other tastes—and hence
This flying-buttress of a nose.

So some genetic memory of tenderness
Where Roman and Briton join
Can on irregular features still impress
The formal profile of a coin.

CLIVE SANSOM

128

Schoolmistress

Miss Humm
Straight-backed as a Windsor chair
She stood on the top playground step
And surveyed her Saturnalian kingdom.
At 8.45 precisely, she stiffened
(If that were possible), produced a key
—A large, cold dungeon-key—
Placed it below her lip, and blew.
No summons from Heaven itself
(It was a church school) was more imperious!
No angel trumpet or Mosean thunder-clap
Calling the Israelites to doom or repentance
Met swifter obedience. No Gorgon
Suspended life with such efficiency.
In the middle of a shout, a scream,
We halted. Our faces froze.
No longer George or Tom or Mary,
But forty reproductions of a single child,
Chilled to conformity. We gathered
Like captive troops and, climbing steps,
Received the inspection of her cool eyes,
Willing them away from unwashed necks
Or black-ringed fingernails,
But knowing our very thoughts were visible
If she chose to see. Nothing escaped her.
She was (as I said, a church school)
God, St Michael, the Recording Angel
And, in our guiltier moments, Lucifer—
A Lucifer in long tweed skirts
And a blouse severely fastened at the neck
By a round cameo that was no ornament
But the outward sign of inward authority.

Even the Rector, when he stepped inside
And the brown walls rumbled to his voice,
Dwindled to a curate . . . .
It would have astonished us to learn, I think,
That she ate supper, went to bed,
And even, perhaps, on occasions, slept.

CLIVE SANSOM

The Place's Fault

Once, after a rotten day at school—
Sweat on my fingers, pages thumbed with smears,
Cane smashing down to make me keep them neat—
I blinked out to the sunlight and the heat
And stumbled up the hill, still swallowing tears.
A stone hissed past my ear—'yah! gurt fat fool!'

Some urchins waited for me by my gate.
I shouted swear-words at them, walked away.
'Yeller', they yelled, ''e's yeller!' And they flung
Clods, stones, bricks—anything to make me run.
I ran, all right, up hill all scorching day
With 'yeller' in my ears. 'I'm not, I'm not!'

Another time, playing too near the shops—
Oddly no doubt, I'm told I was quite odd,
Making, no doubt, a noise—a girl in slacks
Came out and told some kids 'Run round the back,
Bash in his back door, smash up his back yard,
And if he yells I'll go and fetch the cops.'

And what a rush I had to lock those doors
Before that rabble reached them! What desire
I've had these twenty years to lock away
That place where fingers pointed out my play,
Where even the grass was tangled with barbed wire,
Where through the streets I waged continual wars!

We left (it was a temporary halt)
The knots of ragged kids, the wired-off beach,
Faces behind the blinds. I'll not return;
There's nothing there I haven't had to learn,
And I've learned nothing that I'd care to teach—
Except that I know it was the place's fault.

PHILIP HOBSBAUM

The Pay is Good

A class of thirty student engineers,
Sixteen years old, disliked by all the staff.
Hearing about them at the interview,
And told to rule them with a rod of iron,
I tried my best but found I could not laugh.

He might be wrong. But I, no raw recruit,
Had found a proverb in a classroom war:
The peaceful sheriff proves that he can shoot
Before he throws his gunbelt on the floor.

A month or so of brooding self-distrust,
And then the moment came. I reached the door
(So this is it. Fight, for the love of Kell.
Show them who's boss—there's no going back—you must)—
And flung it open on the core of hell.

Somehow it worked. And they will never know
By what dissimulation it was done;
Or how the fuse of terror blasted out
Courage enough to master thirty-one.

RICHARD KELL

132

Fishing Harbour
towards Evening

Slashed clouds leak gold. Along the slurping wharf
The snugged boats creak and seesaw. Round the masts

Abrasive squalls flake seagulls off the sky:
Choppy with wings the rapids of shrill sound.

Wrapt in spliced airs of fish and tar,
Light wincing on their knives, the clockwork men

Incise and scoop the oily pouches, flip
The soft guts overboard with blood-wet fingers.

Among three rhythms the slapping silver turns
To polished icy marble upon the deck.

RICHARD KELL

Sailing to an Island

The boom above my knees lifts, and the boat
Drops, and the surge departs, departs, my cheek
Kissed and rejected, kissed, as the gaff sways
A tangent, cuts the infinite sky to red
Maps, and the mast draws eight and eight across
Measureless blue, the boatmen sing or sleep.

We point all day for our chosen island,
Clare, with its crags purpled by legend:
There under castles the hot O'Malleys,
Daughters of Granuaile, the pirate queen
Who boarded a Turk with a blunderbuss,
Comb red hair and assemble cattle.
Across the shelved Atlantic groundswell
Plumbed by the sun's kingfisher rod,
We sail to locate in sea, earth and stone
The myth of a shrewd and brutal swordswoman
Who piously endowed an abbey.
Seven hours we try against wind and tide,
Tack and return, making no headway.
The north wind sticks like a gag in our teeth.

Encased in a mirage, steam on the water,
Loosely we coast where hideous rocks jag
An acropolis of cormorants, an extinct
Volcano where spiders spin, a purgatory
Guarded by hags and bristled with breakers.

The breeze as we plunge slowly stiffens:
There are hills of sea between us and land,

Between our hopes and the island harbour.
A child vomits. The boat veers and bucks.
There is no refuge on the gannet's cliff.
We are far, far out: the hull is rotten,
The spars are splitting, the rigging is frayed,
And our helmsman laughs uncautiously.
What of those who must earn their living
On the ribald face of a mad mistress?
We in holiday fashion know
This is the boat that belched its crew
Dead on the shingle in the Cleggan disaster.

Now she dips, and the sail hits the water.
She hoves to a squall; is struck; and shudders.
Someone is shouting. The boom, weak as scissors,
Has snapped. The boatman is praying.

Orders thunder and canvas cannonades.
She smothers in spray. We still have a mast;
The oar makes a boom. I am told to cut
Cords out of fishing-lines, fasten the jib.
Ropes lash my cheeks. Ease! Ease at last:
She swings to leeward, we can safely run.
Washed over rails our Clare Island dreams,
With storm behind us we straddle the wakeful
Waters that draw us headfast to Inishbofin.

The bows rock as she overtakes the surge.
We neither sleep nor sing nor talk,
But look to the land where the men are mowing.
What will the islanders think of our folly?

The whispering spontaneous reception committee
Nods and smokes by the calm jetty.
Am I jealous of these courteous fishermen
Who hand us ashore, for knowing the sea
Intimately, for respecting the storm
That took nine of their men on one bad night
And five from Rossadillisk in this very boat?
Their harbour is sheltered. They are slow to tell
The story again. There is local pride
In their home-built ships.
We are advised to return next day by the mail.

But tonight we stay, drinking with people
Happy in the monotony of boats,
Bringing the catch to the Cleggan market,
Cultivating fields, or retiring from America
With enough to soak till morning or old age.

The bench below my knees lifts, and the floor
Drops, and the words depart, depart, with faces
Blurred by the smoke. An old man grips my arm,
His shot eyes twitch, quietly dissatisfied.
He has lost his watch, an American gold
From Boston gas-works. He treats the company
To the secretive surge, the sea of his sadness.
I slip outside, fall among stones and nettles,
Crackling dry twigs on an elder tree,
While an accordion drones above the hill.

Later, I reach a room, where the moon stares
Cob-webbed through the window. The tide has ebbed,
Boats are careened in the harbour. Here is a bed.

RICHARD MURPHY

136

Disturbances

After the darkness has come
And the distant 'planes catch fire
In the dusk, coming home,
And the tall church spire
No longer stands on the hill
And the streets are quiet except
For a car-door slamming—well,
You might say the houses slept.
An owl calls from a tree.

This is my house and home,
A place where for several years
I've settled, to which I've come
Happily, set my shears
To the hedge which fronts the place,
Had decorators in,
Altered a former face
To a shape I can call my own.
An owl calls from a tree.

Only, sometimes at night
Or running downhill for a train,
I suddenly catch sight
Of a world not named and plain
And without hedges or walls:
A jungle of noises, fears,
No lucid intervals,
No calm exteriors.
An owl calls from a tree.

The place I live in has
A name on the map, a date
For all that is or was.
I avoid hunger and hate:
I have a bed for the night:
The dishes are stacked in the rack:
I remember to switch off the light:
I turn and lie on my back.
An owl calls from a tree.

ANTHONY THWAITE

A Sense of Property

After the usual rounds at night
In the house and property called my own,
Front door, back door, bolted tight;
Fire raked down; stove stoked high—
I climbed the stairs and there, alone
On the landing by the nursery,
I saw my daughter watching me.

In fact, a baby in her cot
Asleep, beyond that firm closed door.
But twenty years from now, and not
Our sole sweet charge, our special grace,
She stood like someone glimpsed before
In book or crowd: and in her face
The future marked its time and place.

I knew she was not real, and gone
Within a moment. So I went
Through all the trivial jobs, and on
To bed. But, half asleep, I lay
And wondered how impermanent
The future is, yet day by day
My daughter walks it on its way.

That daughter will not be my own
As house and property are mine,
For in that moment I was shown
A stranger at my baby's door,
A stranger made by some design
Not ours, and hammered out before
She took the shape her mother bore.

But in a curious happiness
I faced that fact, and knew at once
That child and woman would express
Through every known and unknown thing
(Each of them her inheritance)
A permanence in everything,
While acquisitions clog and cling.

She sleeps so light that if I go
Into her room, she turns and stirs.
The house is quiet, its rooms all show
A locked and barred security.
And in my sleep, deeper than hers,
I watch her stand and look at me,
Stripped of possessions and made free.

ANTHONY THWAITE

The Geranium

When I put her out, once, by the garbage pail,
She looked so limp and bedraggled,
So foolish and trusting, like a sick poodle,
Or a wizened aster in late September,
I brought her back in again
For a new routine—
Vitamins, water, and whatever
Sustenance seemed sensible
At the time: she'd lived
So long on gin, bobbie pins, half-smoked cigars, dead beer,
Her shriveled petals falling
On the faded carpet, the stale
Steak grease stuck to her fuzzy leaves.
(Dried-out, she creaked like a tulip.)

The things she endured!—
The dumb dames shrieking half the night
Or the two of us, alone, both seedy,
Me breathing booze at her,
She leaning out of her pot toward the window.

Near the end, she seemed almost to hear me—
And that was scary—
So when that snuffling cretin of a maid
Threw her, pot and all, into the trash-can,
I said nothing.

But I sacked the presumptuous hag the next week,
I was that lonely.

THEODORE ROETHKE

Baking Day

Thursday was baking day in our house.
The spicy smell of new baked bread would meet
My nostrils when I came home from school and there would be
Fresh buns for tea, but better still were the holidays.

Then I could stay and watch the baking of the bread.
My mother would build up the fire and pull out the damper
Until the flames were flaring under the oven; while it was
    heating
She would get out her earthenware bowl and baking board.

Into the crater of flour in the bowl she would pour sugar
And yeast in hot water; to make sure the yeast was fresh
I had often been sent to fetch it from the grocer that morning,
And it smelt of the earth after rain as it dissolved in the sweet
    water.

Then her small stubby hands would knead and pummel
The dough until they became two clowns in baggy pantaloons,
And the right one, whose three fingers and blue stump
Told of the accident which followed my birth, became whole.

As the hands worked a creamy elastic ball
Took shape and covered by a white cloth was set
On a wooden chair by the fire slowly to rise:
To me the most mysterious rite of all.

From time to time I would peep at the living dough
To make sure it was not creeping out of the bowl.
Sometimes I imagined it possessed, filling the whole room,
And we helpless, unable to control its power to grow,

But as it heaved above the rim of the bowl mother
Was there, taking it and moulding it into plaited loaves
And buns and giving me a bit to make into a bread man,
With currant eyes, and I, too, was a baker.

142

My man was baked with the loaves and I would eat him for tea.
On Friday night, when the plaited loaves were placed
Under a white napkin on the dining table,
Beside two lighted candles, they became holy.

No bread will ever be so full of the sun as the pieces
We were given to eat after prayers and the cutting of this
    bread.
My mother, who thought her life had been narrow, did not
    want
Her daughters to be bakers of bread. I think she was wise.

Yet sometimes, when my cultivated brain chafes at kitchen
Tasks, I remember her, patiently kneading dough
And rolling pastry, her untutored intelligence
All bent towards nourishing her children.

ROSEMARY JOSEPH

In the Kitchen
of the Old House

In the kitchen of the old house, late,
I was making some coffee
and I day-dreamed sleepily of old friends.
Then the dream turned. I waited.
I walked alone all day in the town
where I was born. It was cold,
    a Saturday in January
when nothing happens. The streets
    changed as the sky grew dark around me.
The lamps in the small houses
    had tassels on them, and the black cars
at the curb were old and square.
    A ragman passed with his horse, their breaths
blooming like white peonies,
    when I turned into a darker street
and I recognized the house
    from snapshots. I felt as separate
as if the city and the house
    were closed inside a globe which I shook
to make it snow. No sooner
    did I think of snow, but snow started
to fill the heavy darkness
    around me. It reflected the glare
of the streetlight as it fell
    melting on the warmth of the sidewalk
and frozen on frozen grass.
    Then I heard out of the dark the sound
of steps on the bare cement
    in a familiar rhythm. Under
the streetlight, bent to the snow,
    hatless, younger than I, so young that
I was not born, my father
    walked home to his bride and his supper.

A shout gathered inside me
   like a cold wind, to break the rhythm,
to keep him from entering
   that heavy door—but I stood under
a tree, closed in by the snow,
   and did not shout, to tell what happened
in twenty years, in winter,
   when his early death grew inside him
like snow piling on the grass.
   He opened the door and met the young
woman who waited for him.

DONALD HALL

By the Exeter River

'What is it you're mumbling, old Father, my Dad?
Come drink up your soup and I'll put you to bed.'

'By the Exeter River, by the river, I said.'

'Stop dreaming of rivers, old Father, my Dad,
Or save all your dreaming till you're tucked up in bed.'

'It was cold by the river. We came in a sled.'

'It's colder to think of, old Father, my Dad,
Than the blankets and bolsters and pillows of bed.'

'We took off his dress and the cap from his head.'

'Undressed in the winter, old Father, my Dad?
What could you be thinking? Let's get off to bed.'

'And Sally, poor Sally I reckon is dead.'

'Was she an old sweetheart, old Father, my Dad?
Now lean on my shoulder and come up to bed.'

'We drowned your half-brother. I remember we did.'

DONALD HALL

The Old Pilot's Death

He discovers himself on an old airfield.
He thinks he was there before,
but rain has washed out the lettering of a sign.
A single biplane, all struts and wires,
stands in the long grass and wildflowers.
He pulls himself into the narrow cockpit
although his muscles are stiff
and sits like an egg in a nest of canvas.
He sees that the machine gun has rusted.
The glass over the instruments
has broken, and the red arrows are gone
from his gas gauge and his altimeter.
When he looks up, his propeller is turning,
although no one was there to snap it.
He lets out the throttle. The engine catches
and the propeller spins into the wind.
He bumps over holes in the grass,
and he remembers to pull back on the stick.
He rises from the land in a high bounce
which gets higher, and suddenly he is flying again.
He feels the old fear, and rising over the fields
the old gratitude. In the distance, circling
in a beam of late sun like birds migrating,
there are the wings of a thousand biplanes.
He banks and flies to join them.

in memory of Philip Thompson, d. 1960

DONALD HALL

148

Imperialists in Retirement

'I have done the State some service . . .'
Othello
Tender each to the other, gentle
But not to the world which has just now
Snatched back its gifts. Oh fallen, fallen
From your proconsular state! I watch
Perhaps too closely, with too much
Easy pity, the old man's loving
Protective gesture—the old woman
Accepting the arm of a blind man,
Leaning upon it. I look around
At the faded chintz, at china chipped
By so many packings, unpackings.

I listen, too. This part is not so
Easy. He is not resigned. He cries
Aloud for the state he kept. He wants
Privilege still, and power—the long
Moonlit nights of the steamship voyage
Out to a new appointment. Whisky
And bridge and talk of what's to be done—
The phrase again: 'They're children really.'
And he beats with feeble hands against
The immovable door of blindness,
The shut door of the years. 'Live in the
Past,' he says. 'That's the thing. Live in the
Past.' And his wife soothes him, as one would
A child when it's nearly his bedtime.
'One mustn't grumble', she says. 'Times change.'

Her hands are reddened and swollen I
Notice, saying goodnight. Her head shakes.
She stumbles a little in rising.
Tonight she washes up. Tomorrow
She will scrub their kitchen on her knees.
I see, as we go, the look of love
From her to him blind. Then the door shuts.

EDWARD LUCIE-SMITH

149

Digging

Between my finger and my thumb
The squat pen rests; snug as a gun.

Under my window, a clean rasping sound
When the spade sinks into gravelly ground:
My father, digging. I look down

Till his straining rump among the flowerbeds
Bends low, comes up twenty years away
Stooping in rhythm through potato drills
Where he was digging.

The coarse boot nestled on the lug, the shaft
Against the inside knee was levered firmly.
He rooted out tall tops, buried the bright edge deep
To scatter new potatoes that we picked
Loving their cool hardness in our hands.

By God, the old man could handle a spade.
Just like his old man.

My grandfather cut more turf in a day
Than any other man on Toner's bog.
Once I carried him milk in a bottle
Corked sloppily with paper. He straightened up
To drink it, then fell to right away

Nicking and slicing neatly, heaving sods
Over his shoulder, going down and down
For the good turf. Digging.

The cold smell of potato mould, the squelch and slap
Of soggy peat, the curt cuts of an edge
Through living roots awaken in my head.
But I've no spade to follow men like them.

Between my finger and my thumb
The squat pen rests.
I'll dig with it.

SEAMUS HEANEY

150

For a Junior School Poetry Book

The mothers are waiting in the yard.
Here come the children, fresh from school.
The mothers are wearing rumpled skirts.
What prim mouths, what wrinkly cheeks.
The children swirl through the air to them,
trailing satchels and a smell of chalk.

The children are waiting in the yard.
The mothers come stumbling out of school.
The children stare primly at them,
lace their shoes, pat their heads.
The mothers swirl through the air to cars.
The children crossly drive them home.

The mothers are coming.
The children are waiting.
The mothers had eyes that see
boiled eggs, wool, dung and bed.
The children have eyes that saw
owl and mountain and little mole.

CHRISTOPHER MIDDLETON

Bedtime Story

Long long ago when the world was a wild place
Planted with bushes and peopled by apes, our
Mission Brigade was at work in the jungle.
    Hard by the Congo

Once, when a foraging detail was active
Scouting for green-fly, it came on a grey man, the
Last living man, in the branch of a baobab
    Stalking a monkey.

Earlier men had disposed of, for pleasure,
Creatures whose names we scarcely remember—
Zebra, rhinoceros, elephants, wart-hog,
    Lion, rats, deer. But

After the wars had extinguished the cities
Only the wild ones were left, half-naked
Near the Equator: and here was the last one,
    Starved for a monkey.

By then the Mission Brigade had encountered
Hundreds of such men: and their procedure,
History tells us, was only to feed them:
    Find them and feed them;

Those were the orders. And this was the last one.
Nobody knew that he was, but he was. Mud
Caked on his flat grey flanks. He was crouched, half-
    armed with a shaved spear

Glinting beneath broad leaves. When their jaws cut
Swathes through the bark and he saw fine teeth shine,
Round eyes roll round and forked arms waver
    Huge as the rough trunks

Over his head, he was frightened. Our workers
Marched through the Congo before he was born, but
This was the first time perhaps that he'd seen one.
    Staring in hot still

Silence, he crouched there: then jumped. With a long swing
Down from his branch, he had angled his spear too
Quickly, before they could hold him, and hurled it
    Hard at the soldier

Leading the detail. How could he know Queen's
Orders were only to help him? The soldier
Winced when the tipped spear pricked him. Unsheathing his
    Sting was a reflex.

Later the Queen was informed. There were no more
Men. An impetuous soldier had killed off,
Purely by chance, the penultimate primate.
    When she was certain,

Squadrons of workers were fanned through the Congo
Detailed to bring back the man's picked bones to be
Sealed in the archives in amber. I'm quite sure
    Nobody found them

After the most industrious search, though.
Where had the bones gone? Over the earth, dear,
Ground by the teeth of the termites, blown by the
    Wind, like the dodo's.

GEORGE MACBETH

Owl

is my favourite. Who flies
like a nothing through the night,
who-whoing. Is a feather
duster in leafy corners ring-a-rosy-ing
boles of mice. Twice

you hear him call. Who
is he looking for? You hear
him hoovering over the floor
of the wood. O would you be gold
rings in the driving skull

if you could? Hooded and
vulnerable by the winter suns
owl looks. Is the grain of bark
in the dark. Round beaks are at
work in the pellety nest,

resting. Owl is an eye
in the barn. For a hole
in the trunk owl's blood
is to blame. Black talons in the
petrified fur! Cold walnut hands

on the case of the brain! In the reign
of the chicken owl comes like
a god. Is a goad in
the rain to the pink eyes,
dripping. For a meal in the day

flew, killed, on the moor. Six
mouths are the seed of his
arc in the season. Torn meat
from the sky. Owl lives
by the claws of his brain. On the branch

in the sever of the hand's
twigs owl is a backward look.
Flown wind in the skin. Fine
rain in the bones. Owl breaks
like the day. Am an owl, am an owl.

GEORGE MACBETH

Bats

A bat is born
Naked and blind and pale.
His mother makes a pocket of her tail
And catches him. He clings to her long fur
By his thumbs and toes and teeth.
And then the mother dances through the night
Doubling and looping, soaring, somersaulting—
Her baby hangs on underneath.
All night, in happiness, she hunts and flies.
Her high sharp cries
Like shining needlepoints of sound
Go out into the night and, echoing back,
Tell her what they have touched.
She hears how far it is, how big it is,
Which way it's going:
She lives by hearing.
The mother eats the moths and gnats she catches
In full flight; in full flight
The mother drinks the water of the pond
She skims across. Her baby hangs on tight.
Her baby drinks the milk she makes him
In moonlight or starlight, in mid-air.
Their single shadow, printed on the moon
Or fluttering across the stars,
Whirls on all night; at daybreak
The tired mother flaps home to her rafter.
The others all are there.
They hang themselves up by their toes,
They wrap themselves in their brown wings.
Bunched upside-down, they sleep in air.
Their sharp ears, their sharp teeth, their quick sharp
    faces
Are dull and slow and mild.
All the bright day, as the mother sleeps,
She folds her wings about her sleeping child.

RANDALL JARRELL

156

Columbus

To find the Western path,
Right thro' the Gates of Wrath . . .
      —BLAKE

As I walked with my friend,
My singular Columbus,
Where the land comes to an end
And the path is perilous,
Where the wheel and tattered shoe
And bottle have been thrown,
And the sky is shining blue,
And the heart sinks like a stone,

I plucked his sleeve and said,
'I have come far to find
The springs of a broken bed,
The ocean, and the wind.
I'd rather live in Greece,
Castile, or an English town
Than wander here like this
Where the dunes come tumbling down.'

He answered me, 'Perhaps.
But Europe never guessed
America, their maps
Could not describe the West.
And though in Plato's glass
The stars were still and clear,
Yet nothing came to pass
And men died of despair.'

He said, 'If there is not
A way to China, one
City surpassing thought,
My ghost will still go on.
I'll spread the airy sail.'
He said, 'and point the sprit
To a country that cannot fail,
For there's no finding it.'

Straightway we separated—
He, in his fading coat,
To the water's edge, where waited
An admiral's longboat.
A crew of able seamen
Sprang up at his command—
An angel or a demon—
And they rowed him from the land.

LOUIS SIMPSON

Geography Lesson

When the jet sprang into the sky,
it was clear why the city
had developed the way it had,
seeing it scaled six inches to the mile.
There seemed an inevitability
about what on ground had looked haphazard,
unplanned and without style
when the jet sprang into the sky.

When the jet reached ten thousand feet,
it was clear why the country
had cities where rivers ran
and why the valleys were populated.
The logic of geography—
that land and water attracted man—
was clearly delineated
when the jet reached ten thousand feet.

When the jet rose six miles high,
it was clear that the earth was round
and that it had more sea than land.
But it was difficult to understand
that the men on the earth found
causes to hate each other, to build
walls across cities and to kill.
From that height, it was not clear why.

ZULFIKAR GHOSE

Warning

When I am an old woman I shall wear purple
With a red hat which doesn't go, and doesn't suit me,
And I shall spend my pension on brandy and summer gloves
And satin sandals, and say we've no money for butter.
I shall sit down on the pavement when I'm tired
And gobble up samples in shops and press alarm bells
And run my stick along the public railings
And make up for the sobriety of my youth.
I shall go out in my slippers in the rain
And pick the flowers in other people's gardens
And learn to spit.

You can wear terrible shirts and grow more fat
And eat three pounds of sausages at a go
Or only bread and pickle for a week
And hoard pens and pencils and beermats and things in boxes.

But now we must have clothes that keep us dry
And pay the rent and not swear in the street
And set a good example for the children.
We must have friends to dinner and read the papers.

But maybe I ought to practise a little now?
So people who know me are not too shocked and surprised
When suddenly I am old and start to wear purple.

JENNY JOSEPH

Mmenson

Summon now the kings of the forest,
horn of the elephant,
mournful call of the elephant;

summon the emirs, kings of the desert,
horses caparisoned, beaten gold bent,
archers and criers, porcupine arrows, bows bent;

recount now the gains and the losses:
Agades, Sokoto, El Hassan dead in his tent,
the silks and the brasses, the slow weary tent

of our journeys down slopes, dry river courses;
land of the lion, land of the leopard, elephant
country; tall grasses, thick prickly herbs. Blow elephant

trumpet; summon the horses,
dead horses, our losses: the bent
slow bow of the Congo, the watering Niger . . .

mmenson: an orchestra of seven elephant-tusk horns,
used on state occasions to relate history.

EDWARD BRATHWAITE

Chad

This sacred lake
is the soul
of the world;

winds whirl
born in the soul
of this dark water's world.

This lake
moulds
the wars of the world;

no peace in this world
till the soul
knows this dark water's

world.
Reeds whisper
here in the morning;

buffaloes blaze;
and around these shores,
man whirls

in his dark rest-
less haste; search-
ing for hope; seek-

ing his fate
far from the shores
of this lake.

EDWARD BRATHWAITE

Timbuctu

Whose gold you carry, camel,
in this cold cold world?
Whose pearls of great price?
Whose cinnamon, whose spice

Your world of walls, o city
of my birth, rises so certain
so secure; the plains
of dust surrounding us

so kept away, so distant.
Whose gold you carry, camel,
on your hill-top back?
To what far land you now

transport our wealth?
And what wealth here, what
riches, when the gold returns
to dust, the walls

we raised return again
to dust; and what sharp winds,
teeth'd with the desert's sand,
rise in the sun's dry

brilliance where our mosques
mock ignorance, mock pride,
burn in the crackled blaze of time,
return again to whispers, dust.

EDWARD BRATHWAITE

Sunstrike

A solitary prospector
staggered, locked in a vision
of slate hills that capered
on the molten horizon.

Waterless, he came to where
a river had run, now a band
flowing only in ripples
of white unquenchable sand.

Cursing, he dug sporadically
here, here, as deep as his arm,
and sat quite still, eyes thirstily
incredulous on his palm.

A handful of alluvial
diamonds leered back, and more: mixed
in the scar, glinted globules
of rubies, emeralds, onyx.

And then he was swimming in fire
and drinking, splashing hot halos
of glittering drops at the choir
of assembled carrion crows.

DOUGLAS LIVINGSTONE

A River

In Madurai,
            city of temples and poets
who sang of cities and temples:

every summer
a river dries to a trickle
in the sand,
baring the sand-ribs,
straw and women's hair
clogging the watergates
at the rusty bars
under the bridges with patches
of repair all over them,
the wet stones glistening like sleepy
crocodiles, the dry ones
shaven water-buffaloes lounging in the sun.

The poets sang only of the floods.

He was there for a day
when they had the floods.
People everywhere talked
of the inches rising,
of the precise number of cobbled steps
run over by the water, rising
on the bathing places,
and the way it carried off three village houses,
one pregnant woman
and a couple of cows
named Gopi and Brinda, as usual.

The new poets still quoted
the old poets, but no one spoke
in verse
of the pregnant woman
drowned, with perhaps twins in her,
kicking at blank walls
even before birth.

He said:
the river has water enough
to be poetic
about only once a year
and then
it carries away
in the first half-hour
three village houses,
a couple of cows
named Gopi and Brinda
and one pregnant woman
expecting identical twins
with no moles on their bodies,
with different-coloured diapers

to tell them apart.

A. K. RAMANUJAN

Song of
the Banana Man

Touris', white man, wipin' his face,
Met me in Golden Grove market place.
He looked at m' ol' clothes brown wid stain,
An' soaked right through wid de Portlan' rain,
He cas' his eye, turn' up his nose,
He says, 'You're a beggar man, I suppose?'
He says, 'Boy, get some occupation,
Be of some value to your nation.'

I said, 'By God and dis big right han'
You mus' recognize a banana man.

'Up in de hills where de streams are cool,
An' mullet an' janga swim in de pool,
I have ten acres of mountain side,
An' a dainty-foot donkey dat I ride,
Four Gros Michel, an' four Lacatan,
Some coconut trees, an' some hills of yam,
An' I pasture on dat very same lan'
Five she-goats an' a big black ram,

'Dat, by God an' dis big right han'
Is de property of a banana man.

'I leave m'yard early-mornin' time
An' set m' foot to de mountain climb,
I ben' m' back to de hot-sun toil,
An' m' cutlass rings on de stony soil,
Ploughin' an' weedin', diggin' an' plantin'
Till Massa Sun drop back o' John Crow mountain,
Den home again in cool evenin' time,
Perhaps whistlin' dis likkle rhyme,

(SUNG) 'Praise God an' m' big right han'
I will live and die a banana man.

'Banana day is my special day,
I cut my stems an' I'm on m' way,
Load up de donkey, leave de lan'
Head down de hill to banana stan'.
When de truck comes roun', I take a ride
All de way down to de harbour side—
Dat is de night, when you, touris' man,
Would change your place wid a banana man.

'Yes, by God, an' m' big right han'
I will live and die a banana man.

'De bay is calm, an' de moon is bright,
De hills look black though the sky is light,
Down at de dock is an English ship,
Restin' after her ocean trip,
While on de pier is a monstrous hustle,
Tallymen, carriers, all in a bustle,
Wid stems on deir heads in a long black snake
Some singing de songs dat banana men make

'Like, (SUNG) 'Praise God an' m' big right han'
I will live an' die a banana man.

'Den de payment comes, an' we have some fun,
Me, Zekiel, Breda an' Duppy Son.
Down at de bar near United Wharf
We knock back a white rum, burs' a laugh,
Fill de empty bag for further toil
Wid saltfish, breadfruit, coconut oil.
Den head back home to m' yard to sleep,
A proper sleep dat is long an' deep.

'Yes, by God an' m' big right han'
I will live an' die a banana man.

'So when you see dese ol' clothes brown wid stain,
An' soaked right through wid de Portlan' rain,
Don't cas' your eye, nor turn your nose,
Don't judge a man by his patchy clothes,
I'm a strong man, a proud man, an' I'm free,
Free as dese mountains, free as dis sea,
I know myself, an' I know m' ways
An' will sing wid pride till de end o' m' days,

(SUNG) 'Praise God an' m' big right han'
I will live an' die a banana man.'

EVAN JONES

Lament
of the Banana Man

Gal, I'm tellin' you, I'm tired fo' true,
Tired of Englan', tired o' you.
But I can' go back to Jamaica now . . . .

I'm here in Englan', I'm drawin' pay,
I go to de underground every day—
Eight hours is all, half-hour fo' lunch,
M' uniform's free, an' m' ticket punch—
Punchin' tickets not hard to do,
When I'm tired o' punchin', I let dem through.

I get a paid holiday once a year.
Ol' age an' sickness can' touch me here.

I have a room o' m' own, an' a iron bed,
Dunlopillo under m' head,
A Morphy-Richards to warm de air,
A formica table, an easy chair.
I have summer clothes, an' winter clothes,
An' paper kerchiefs to blow m' nose.

My yoke is easy, my burden is light,
I know a place I can go to, any night.
Dis place Englan'! I'm not complainin',
If it col', it col', if it rainin', it rainin'.
I don' min' if it's mostly night,
Dere's always inside, or de sodium light.

I don' min' white people starin' at me
Dey don' want me here? Don't is deir country?
You won' catch me bawlin' any homesick tears
If I don' see Jamaica for a t'ousand years!

. . . Gal, I'm tellin' you, I'm tired fo' true,
Tired of Englan', tired o' you,
I can' go back to Jamaica now—
But I'd want to die there, anyhow.

EVAN JONES

Eve to her Daughters

It was not I who began it.
Turned out into draughty caves,
hungry so often, having to work for our bread,
hearing the children whining,
I was nevertheless not unhappy.
Where Adam went I was fairly contented to go.
I adapted myself to the punishment: it was my life.

But Adam, you know . . . !
He kept on brooding over the insult,
over the trick They had played on us, over the scolding.
He had discovered a flaw in himself
and he had to make up for it.
Outside Eden the earth was imperfect,
the seasons changed, the game was fleet-footed,
he had to work for our living, and he didn't like it.
He even complained of my cooking
(it was hard to compete with Heaven).

So, he set to work.
The earth must be made a new Eden
with central heating, domesticated animals,
mechanical harvesters, combustion engines,
escalators, refrigerators,
and modern means of communication
and multiplied opportunities for safe investment
and higher education for Abel and Cain
and the rest of the family.
You can see how his pride had been hurt.

In the process he had to unravel everything,
because he believed that mechanism
was the whole secret—he was always mechanical-minded.
He got to the very inside of the whole machine
exclaiming as he went, So this is how it works!

And now that I know how it works, why, I must have
    invented it.
As for God and the Other, they cannot be demonstrated,
and what cannot be demonstrated
doesn't exist.
You see, he had always been jealous.

Yes, he got to the centre
where nothing at all can be demonstrated.
And clearly he doesn't exist; but he refuses
to accept the conclusion.
You see, he was always an egotist.

It was warmer than this in the cave;
there was none of this fall-out.
I would suggest, for the sake of the children,
that it's time you took over.

But you are my daughters, you inherit my own faults of
    character;
you are submissive, following Adam
even beyond existence.
Faults of character have their own logic
and it always works out.
I observed this with Abel and Cain.

Perhaps the whole elaborate fable
right from the beginning
is meant to demonstrate this; perhaps it's the whole secret.
Perhaps nothing exists but our faults?

But it's useless to make
such a suggestion to Adam.
He has turned himself into God,
who is faultless, and doesn't exist.

JUDITH WRIGHT

Spicer's Instant Poetry

On sale everywhere: Spicer's Instant Poetry.
Trial size, 2/-; epic pack, 19/6.
A balanced mixture of clichés, catchwords,
Symbols, non sequiturs, ambiguities,
Stock phrases and borrowings from the best models.
Warranted free from superfluous emotion,
Bad rhymes and obvious plagiarism.
Simply add luke-warm milk and water.
A child can use it.
One teaspoonful reconstitutes a sonnet.
This infallible preparation
Makes poems suitable for competitions,
National and international festivals,
Private greetings cards and autograph albums.
Results guaranteed, and are to be seen
In best literary journals.
Spicer's Instant Poetry comes in seven popular shades:
Nature (including animals), childhood, domestic troubles,
Industry and politics, thwarted love,
Mythology and religion, foreign parts.
Special 'Parnassus' kit containing all the above varieties,
Free surprise item and coloured art portrait of leading bard,
Or 'Tartan Special' for Scottish subjects,
Five shillings only, post free.
Extra strong mix for homosexual or surgical pieces.
Delighted user writes: 'Instant Poetry
Is a joy for ever . . . Indistinguishable from the real thing.'
Order now and astonish your friends.
Big cash opportunities: Immortality
Assured or money returned.

JAMES REEVES

174

Rythm

They dunno how it is. I smack a ball
right through the goals. But they dunno how the words
get muddled in my head, get tired somehow.
I look through the window, see. And there's a wall
I'd kick the ball against, just smack and smack.
Old Jerry he can't play, he don't know how,
not now at any rate. He's too flicking small.
See him in shorts, out in the crazy black.
Rythm, he says, and ryme. See him at back.
He don't know nuthing about Law. He'd fall
flat on his face, just like a big sack,
when you're going down the wing, the wind behind you
and crossing into the goalmouth and they're roaring
the whole great crowd. They're up on their feet cheering.
The ball's at your feet and there it goes, just crack.
Old Jerry dives—the wrong way. And they're jearing
and I run to the centre and old Bash
jumps up and down, and I feel great, and wearing
my gold and purpel strip, fresh from the wash.

IAIN CRICHTON SMITH

Autumn

It is the football season once more
And the back pages of the Sunday papers
Again show the blurred anguish of goalkeepers.

In Maida Vale, Golders Green and Hampstead
Lamps ripen early in the surprising dusk;
They are furred like stale rinds with a fuzz of mist.

The pavements of Kensington are greasy;
The wind smells of burnt porridge in Bayswater,
And the leaves are mushed to silence in the gutter.

The big hotel like an anchored liner
Rides near the park; lit windows hammer the sky.
Like the slow swish of surf the tyres of taxis sigh.

On Ealing Broadway the cinema glows
Warm behind glass while mellow the church clock
    chimes
As the waiting girls stir in their delicate chains.

Their eyes are polished by the wind,
But the gleam is dumb, empty of joy or anger.
Though the lovers are long in coming the girls still
    linger.

We are nearing the end of the year.
Under the sombre sleeve the blood ticks faster
And in the dark ear of Autumn quick voices whisper.

It is a time of year that's to my taste,
Full of spiced rumours, sharp and velutinous flavours,
Dim with the mist that softens the cruel surfaces,
Makes mirrors vague. It is the mist that I most favour.

VERNON SCANNELL

Cornish Cliffs

Those moments, tasted once and never done,
Of long surf breaking in the mid-day sun,
A far-off blow-hole booming like a gun—

The seagulls plane and circle out of sight
Below this thirsty, thrift-encrusted height,
The veined sea-campion buds burst into white

And gorse turns tawny orange, seen beside
Pale drifts of primroses cascading wide
To where the slate falls sheer into the tide.

More than in gardened Surrey, nature spills
A wealth of heather, kidney-vetch and squills
Over these long-defended Cornish hills.

A gun-emplacement of the latest war
Looks older than the hill fort built before
Saxon or Norman headed for the shore.

And in the shadowless, unclouded glare
Deep blue above us fades to whiteness where
A misty sea-line meets the wash of air.

Nut-smell of gorse and honey-smell of ling
Waft out to sea the freshness of the spring
On sunny shallows, green and whispering.

The wideness which the lark-song gives the sky
Shrinks at the clang of sea-birds sailing by
Whose notes are tuned to days when seas are high.

From today's calm, the lane's enclosing green
Leads inland to a usual Cornish scene—
Slate cottages with sycamore between,

Small fields and tellymasts and wires and poles
With, as the everlasting ocean rolls,
Two chapels built for half a hundred souls.

JOHN BETJEMAN

The Force

At Mrs Tyson's farmhouse, the electricity is pumped
Off her beck-borne wooden wheel outside.
Greased, steady, it spins within
A white torrent, that stretches up the rocks.
At night its force bounds down
And shakes the lighted rooms, shakes the light;
The mountain's force comes towering down to us.

High near its summit the brink is hitched
To an overflowing squally tarn.
It trembles with stored storms
That pulse across the rim to us, as light.

On a gusty day like this the force
Lashes its tail, the sky abounds
With wind-stuffed rinds of cloud that sprout
Clear force, throbbing in squalls off the sea
Where the sun stands poring down at itself
And makes the air grow tall in spurts
Whose crests turn over in the night-wind, foaming. We
    spin
Like a loose wheel, and throbbing shakes our light
Into winter, and torrents dangle. Sun
Pulls up the air in fountains, green shoots, forests
Flinching up at it in spray of branches,
Sends down clear water and the loosened torrent
Down into Mrs Tyson's farmhouse backyard,
That pumps white beams off its crest,
In a stiff breeze lashes its tail down the rocks.

PETER REDGROVE

178

Thistles

Against the rubber tongues of cows and the hoeing
   hands of men
Thistles spike the summer air
Or crackle open under a blue-black pressure.

Every one a revengeful burst
Of resurrection, a grasped fistful
Of splintered weapons and Icelandic frost thrust up

From the underground stain of a decayed Viking.
They are like pale hair and the gutturals of dialects.
Every one manages a plume of blood.

Then they grow grey, like men.
Mown down, it is a feud. Their sons appear,
Stiff with weapons, fighting back over the same ground.

TED HUGHES

Touch

You are already
asleep. I lower
myself in next to
you, my skin slightly
numb with the restraint
of habits, the patina of
self, the black frost
of outsideness, so that even
unclothed it is
a resilient chilly
hardness, a superficially
malleable, dead
rubbery texture.

You are a mound
of bedclothes, where the cat
in sleep braces
its paws against your
calf through the blankets,
and kneads each paw in turn.

Meanwhile and slowly
I feel a is it
my own warmth surfacing or
the ferment of your whole
body that in darkness beneath
the cover is stealing
bit by bit to break
down that chill.

You turn and
hold me tightly, do
you know who
I am or am I
your mother or
the nearest human being to
hold on to in a
dreamed pogrom.

What I, now loosened,
sink into is an old
big place, it is
there already, for
you are already
there, and the cat
got there before you, yet
it is hard to locate.
What is more, the place is
not found but seeps
from our touch in
continuous creation, dark
enclosing cocoon round
ourselves alone, dark
wide realm where we
walk with everyone.

THOM GUNN

At Dunwich

Fifteen churches lie here
Under the North Sea;
Forty-five years ago
The last went down the cliff.
You can see, at low tide,
A mound of masonry
Chewed like a damp bun.

In the village now (if you call
Dunwich a village now,
With a handful of houses, one street,
And a shack for Tizer and tea)
You can ask an old man
To show you the stuff they've found
On the beach when there's been a storm:

Knife-blades, buckles and rings,
Enough coins to fill an old sock,
Badges that men wore
When they'd been on pilgrimage,
Armfuls of broken pots.
People cut bread, paid cash,
Buttoned up against the cold.

Fifteen churches, and men
In thousands working at looms,
And wives brewing up stews
In great grey cooking pots.
I put out a hand and pull
A sherd from the cliff's jaws.
The sand trickles, then falls.

Nettles grow on the cliffs
In clumps as high as a house.
The houses have gone away.
Stand and look at the sea
Eating the land as it walks
Steadily treading the tops
Of fifteen churches' spires.

ANTHONY THWAITE

Above Penmaenmawr

The upland farmers have all gone;
the lane they laid twists without purpose,
visiting broken gates and overgrown
gardens, to end in clumps of gorse.

Their unroofed houses, and fallen barns,
rich in nettles, lie dead in hiding
from the wind that howls off Talyfan's
saw-tooth ridge; their walls divide

bracken from bracken; their little church
of bare rock has outlasted use:
hikers' signatures in the porch,
'Keys obtainable at the Guesthouse'.

Yet, not to sentimentalize,
their faces turned from drudgery
when the chance showed itself. There is
hardly a sign of the husbandry

of even the last to leave—so slight
was their acceptance by the land.
They left for the seaside towns, to get
easier jobs, and cash in hand.

Five miles of uplands, and beyond—
a thousand feet below—the coast,
its bright lights twinkling; freezing wind
dragging the cloud down like a frost

from Talyfan. Alone upon
these darkening, silent heights, my fears
stay stubbornly with the farmers, gone
after six hundred thankless years.

TONY CONNOR

184

Aunt Julia

Aunt Julia spoke Gaelic
very loud and very fast.
I could not answer her—
I could not understand her.

She wore men's boots
when she wore any.
—I can see her strong foot,
stained with peat,
paddling the treadle of the spinningwheel
while her right hand drew yarn
marvellously out of the air.

Hers was the only house
where I lay at night
in the absolute darkness
of the box bed, listening to
crickets being friendly.

She was buckets
and water flouncing into them.
She was winds pouring wetly
round house-ends.
She was brown eggs, black skirts
and a keeper of threepennybits
in a teapot.

Aunt Julia spoke Gaelic
very loud and very fast.
By the time I had learned
a little, she lay
silenced in the absolute black
of a sandy grave

at Luskentyre.
But I hear her still, welcoming me
with a seagull's voice
across a hundred yards
of peatscrapes and lazybeds
and getting angry, getting angry
with so many questions
unanswered.

NORMAN MACCAIG

Uncle Roderick

His drifter swung in the night
from a mile of nets
between the Shiants and Harris.

My boy's eyes watched
the lights of the fishing fleet—fireflies
on the green field of the sea.

In the foc's'le he gave me a bowl
of tea, black, strong and bitter,
and a biscuit you hammered
in bits like a plate.

The fiery curtain came up
from the blackness, comma'd with corpses.

Round Rhu nan Cuideagan
he steered for home, a boy's god
in seaboots. He found his anchorage
as a bird its nest.

In the kitchen he dropped
his oilskins where he stood.

He was strong as the red bull.
He moved like a dancer.
He was a cran of songs.

NORMAN MACCAIG

An Addition
to the Family: for M.L.

A musical poet, collector of basset-horns,
was buttering his toast down in Dunbartonshire
when suddenly from behind the breakfast newspaper
the shining blade stopped scraping
and he cried to his wife, 'Joyce, listen to this!—
"Two basset-hounds for sale, house-trained, keen
    hunters"—
Oh we must have them! What d'you think?' 'But dear,
did you say *hounds*?' 'Yes yes, hounds, hounds—'
'But Maurice, it's *horns* we want, you must be over
in the livestock column, you can't play a hound!'
'It's Beverley it says, the kennels are at Beverley—'
'But Maurice—' '—I'll get some petrol, we'll be there by
    lunchtime—'
'But a dog, two dogs, where'll we put them?'
'I've often wondered what these dogs are like—'
'You mean you don't even—' 'Is there no more
    marmalade?'
'—don't know what they look like? And how are we to
    feed them?
Yes, there's the pot dear.' 'This stuff's all peel, isn't it?'
'Well, we're at the end of it. But look, these two great—'
'You used to make marmalade once upon a time.'
'They've got ears down to here, and they're far too—'
'Is that half past eight? I'll get the car out.
See if I left my cheque-book on the—' 'Maurice,
are you mad? What about your horns?' 'What horns,
what are you talking about? Look Joyce dear,
if it's not on the dresser it's in my other jacket.
I believe they're wonderful for rabbits—'

So the musical poet took his car to Beverley
with his wife and his cheque-book, and came back home
with his wife and his cheque-book and two new hostages
to the unexpectedness of fortune.
The creatures scampered through the grass, the children
came out with cries of joy, there seemed to be nothing
dead or dying in all that landscape.
Fortune bless the unexpected cries!
Life gathers to the point of wishing it,
a mocking pearl of many ventures. The house
rolled on its back and kicked its legs in the air.
And later, wondering farmers as they passed would hear
behind the lighted window in the autumn evening
two handsome mellow-bosomed basset-hounds
howling to a melodious basset-horn.

EDWIN MORGAN

190

Trio

Coming up Buchanan Street, quickly, on a sharp winter
    evening
a young man and two girls, under the Christmas lights—
The young man carries a new guitar in his arms,
the girl on the inside carries a very young baby,
and the girl on the outside carries a chihuahua.
And the three of them are laughing, their breath rises
in a cloud of happiness, and as they pass
the boy says, 'Wait till he sees this but!'
The chihuahua has a tiny Royal Stewart tartan coat like a
    teapot-holder,
the baby in its white shawl is all bright eyes and mouth like
    favours in a fresh sweet cake,
the guitar swells out under its milky plastic cover, tied at
    the neck with silver tinsel tape and a brisk sprig of
    mistletoe.
Orphean sprig! Melting baby! Warm chihuahua!
The vale of tears is powerless before you.
Whether Christ is born, or is not born, you
put paid to fate, it abdicates
                under the Christmas lights.
Monsters of the year
go blank, are scattered back,
can't bear this march of three.

—And the three have passed, vanished in the crowd
(yet not vanished, for in their arms they wind
the life of men and beasts, and music,
laughter ringing them round like a guard)
at the end of this winter's day.

EDWIN MORGAN

Tonight at Noon*

(for Charles Mingus and the Clayton Squares)

Tonight at noon
Supermarkets will advertise 3d EXTRA on everything
Tonight at noon
Children from happy families will be sent to live in a home
Elephants will tell each other human jokes
America will declare peace on Russia
World War I generals will sell poppies in the streets on
    November 11th
The first daffodils of autumn will appear
When the leaves fall upwards to the trees

Tonight at noon
Pigeons will hunt cats through city backyards
Hitler will tell us to fight on the beaches and on the landing
    fields
A tunnel full of water will be built under Liverpool
Pigs will be sighted flying in formation over Woolton
and Nelson will not only get his eye back but his arm as well
White Americans will demonstrate for equal rights
in front of the Black House
and the Monster has just created Dr Frankenstein

*The title for this poem is taken from an L.P. by Charles
Mingus 'Tonight at Noon', Atlantic 1416.

Girls in bikinis are moonbathing
Folksongs are being sung by real folk
Artgalleries are closed to people over 21
Poets get their poems in the Top 20
Politicians are elected to insane asylums
There's jobs for everyone and nobody wants them
In back alleys everywhere teenage lovers are kissing
in broad daylight

In forgotten graveyards everywhere the dead will quietly
bury the living
and
You will tell me you love me
Tonight at noon

ADRIAN HENRI

193

From Jazz for Five

3: *Colin Barnes, Drums*

Listen listen
There's walking in the world
All those feet
Your feet and mine;

Listen to the child's feet
Brushing on sand
Running on pebbles

They were once our feet
Your feet and mine

Listen to the quick feet
Dancing on wood
Heels tapping his feet
Toes tapping her feet

They were once our feet
Your feet and mine

Walking and running feet
Thumping and slurring feet
Light feet and heavy feet
Your feet, mine;

Keep the feet moving
Quick feet and slow feet
Your feet and my feet
Don't let them stop

Keep the feet moving
Your feet and my feet
Don't let them
Don't let them

JOHN SMITH

194

From Jazz for Five

5: *Shake Keane, Trumpet*

Have you ever heard the sun in the sky
Man have you heard it?
Have you heard it break the black of the night
Man have you heard it?

Have you heard it shouting its songs, have you heard
It scorch up the air like a phoenix bird,
Have you heard the sun singing?

Have you ever heard a man as black
As the blue of night
When he walks with the moon slung over his back
Through the moss blue night?

Have you heard a man like night light all
The world with the flames of a trumpet call
Like the sun gone spinning?

Listen, for a man like a black sun walks
And the green world blazes;
The earth is on fire where a gold man stalks
With his trumpet like a red sun singing its praises.

JOHN SMITH

Conversation with a Giraffe at Dusk in the Zoo

Hail, lofty,
necking quizzically
through the topgallant leaves
with your lady.

No good making eyelashes at
the distance from me to you
though I confess I should like
to caress your tender horns
and toboggan down your neck,
perhaps swing on your tail.

Your dignity fools no one,
you get engagingly awkward
when you separate and collapse
yourself to drink;
and have you seen
yourself cantering?

Alright, alright, I know
I'm ugly standing still,
squat–necked, so–high.

Just remember there's one or two
things about you too, hey,
like, like, birds now;
they fly much higher.

DOUGLAS LIVINGSTONE

Saturday in New York

on saturday on saturday
people look at elephants in
the children's zoo
they look at tigers
and at yaks
they eat peanuts and candy

poverty is personal
said the four cripples

don't feed or annoy
the animals
don't put garbage in the street
the sky is the same colour
even in Harlem

slums have gotten worse
said the democratic candidate

hurry across Central Park
hurry down Broadway
don't look at your neighbour
he may be Puerto Rican
he may want to rape you
don't feed or annoy
the communists

the wind blows ice from the sea
said the old lady in the wheel chair

ANNE BERESFORD

The Romanies in Town

let us leave this place, brother
it is not for us
they have built a great city
with broken glass
see how it shimmers in the evening light?

their feet are bleeding
through walking on splinters
they pretend not to notice

they have offered us a house
with cabbages in the garden
they tell us of their strange country
and want us to stay
and help them fight for it

do not listen, brother
they will bind you with promises
and with hope
on all sides stretch fields of rubble
they say we should admire the view

the young are busy building
new glass palaces
they gather up the splinters
and bathe their feet with tears

come quick come quick
we will take the road towards the sea
we will pick blackberries
from hedges in the lanes
we will pitch camp on empty moors
and watch the hawk skimming
above the trees

but if we do not fight
the hawks will die, sister
they have no time for wild birds
and will shoot us down

ANNE BERESFORD

Missionary

A harsh entry I had of it, Grasud;
the tiny shuttle strained to its limits
by radiation-belts, dust-storms,
not to mention the pitiless heat which
hit it on plunging into the atmosphere
—its fire-shield clean vaporized; and then,
on landing, the utter cold and stillness
of a mountain-slope, cedar-trees and
what they call
snow. As I went numbly through the
routine I could do in my sleep—
mentalizing myself, smothering
my body and the shuttle in a
defensive neutrino-screen, hiding them
securely in the snow,
I looked up and, between the branches
of the cedars, could see
the mother-ship sliding away through
the dark, like an unfixed star, westwards
to its other destinations: that was
the worst moment of all, Grasud! I'd have
called it back! So lonely, such an alien
world they'd left me in. Goodbye, Lagash!
goodbye, Theremon! fare well! (But no
voice now even to make a gesture against
the silence.)
                Then the agonizingly slow
descent, towards the village,
my spirit dark, already missing
not only Theremon and Lagash, but
that other friend, my body's familiar
chemistry. By now I felt my
vaunted courage ebbing, Grasud; I think
those years of training

alone forced me to go on, into the village,
into the houses, inns, into
—after much vain searching—a ripened
womb; there superseding
(not without a pang) its foetus-spirit.
How black that airlock,
after the six suns of our own system,
I needn't tell you. Even space,
in recollection, seemed a blaze of
supernovas. But I settled to my task,
wrestling to get on terms with carbon
compounds fearsomely different from
the synthetic ones I'd practised in.
Of course, as I was born and the years
passed, it seemed as natural to go
on man's two legs as on our Vardian
limbs. But when these pains eased,
one far bitterer grew: my seeds were cast
on stony ground; the more
I exhorted,
—the more I spoke, obliquely, of
the many mansions of our Vardian
Commonwealth, and of the place
that could be theirs—the more it
seemed those simple, instinctive creatures
lied, stole, slandered, fornicated,
killed. . . . Grasud, how often, sick with
failure, only the words of Vrak
sustained me—'a world lies in your hands.'
That was the time he
sent for the three of us when
all ears were ringing with the news of
the three life-planets found in
NDT 1065. If we had hopes,
we masked them. His words to us, for
all that's happened, I'll hoard always.

200

'Thoorin, Lagash, Theremon,' I hear him
saying, 'I'm sending *you* . . . . you're young,
but this is what you've trained for, bio-
enlightenment. You've done well.'
And then—'a world lies in your hands.'
So, Grasud, I toiled. In the end
I tried too hard; the time of space-
rendezvous was almost come. Anyway,
they killed me. I loved them, and they
killed me.
        Yes, it was hard,
as you can well imagine,
on the return-journey, to avoid feeling
the faintest warp of
jealousy, as Theremon and
Lagash talked with
the happy emissaries of their
planets.—What does Vrak say? He is
kind, promises—after this loathsome
rest—another
chance, though not of course on that
planet. My 'inability' (he avoids
the word failure) to raise them
ethically to the point where we could
safely announce ourselves, proves, he
says, there's no point trying again
for a few thousand years. Meanwhile,
he suggests, maybe some of my words
will start to bear fruit . . . . He is kind!
His last words were 'Forget about it,
Thoorin; enjoy your stay on
Atar.' Forget!
with the relaxed faces of my friends a
perpetual thorn!

D. M. THOMAS

201

A Dream of Hanging

He rang me up
In a dream,
My brother did.
He had been hanged
That morning,
Innocent,
And I had slept
Through the striking
Of the clock
While it had taken place,
Eight,
Just about time enough
For it to happen.
He spoke to me
On the telephone
That afternoon
To reassure me,
My dear brother
Who had killed nobody,
And I asked him,
Long distance,
What it had felt like
To be hanged.
'Oh, don't worry, lovey', he said,
'When your time comes.
It tickled rather.'

PATRICIA BEER

Ballad of the Bread Man

Mary stood in the kitchen
Baking a loaf of bread.
An angel flew in through the window.
We've a job for you, he said.

God in his big gold heaven,
Sitting in his big blue chair,
Wanted a mother for his little son.
Suddenly saw you there.

Mary shook and trembled,
It isn't true what you say.
Don't say that, said the angel.
The baby's on its way.

Joseph was in the workshop
Planing a piece of wood.
The old man's past it, the neighbours said.
That girl's been up to no good.

And who was that elegant feller,
They said, in the shiny gear?
The things they said about Gabriel
Were hardly fit to hear.

Mary never answered,
Mary never replied.
She kept the information,
Like the baby, safe inside.

It was election winter.
They went to vote in town.
When Mary found her time had come
The hotels let her down.

The baby was born in an annex
Next to the local pub.
At midnight, a delegation
Turned up from the Farmers' Club.

They talked about an explosion
That cracked a hole in the sky,
Said they'd been sent to the Lamb & Flag
To see god come down from on high.

A few days later a bishop
And a five-star general were seen
With the head of an African country
In a bullet-proof limousine.

We've come, they said, with tokens
For the little boy to choose.
Told the tale about war and peace
In the television news.

After them came the soldiers
With rifle and bomb and gun,
Looking for enemies of the state.
The family had packed and gone.

When they got back to the village
The neighbours said, to a man,
That boy will never be one of us,
Though he does what he blessed well can.

He went round to all the people
A paper crown on his head.
Here is some bread from my father.
Take, eat, he said.

Nobody seemed very hungry.
Nobody seemed to care.
Nobody saw the god in himself
Quietly standing there.

He finished up in the papers.
He came to a very bad end.
He was charged with bringing the living to life.
No man was that prisoner's friend.

There's only one kind of punishment
To fit that kind of a crime.
They rigged a trial and shot him dead.
They were only just in time.

They lifted the young man by the leg,
They lifted him by the arm,
They locked him in a cathedral
In case he came to harm.

They stored him safe as water
Under seven rocks.
One Sunday morning he burst out
Like a jack-in-the-box.

Through the town he went walking.
He showed them the holes in his head.
Now do you want any loaves? he cried.
Not today, they said.

CHARLES CAUSLEY

Adrian Henri's Talking After Christmas Blues

Well I woke up this mornin' it was Christmas Day
And the birds were singing the night away
I saw my stocking lying on the chair
Looked right to the bottom but you weren't there
there was
        apples
         oranges
          chocolates
            . . . . aftershave
—but no you.

So I went downstairs and the dinner was fine
There was pudding and turkey and lots of wine
And I pulled those crackers with a laughing face
Till I saw there was no one in your place
there was
        mincepies
         brandy
          nuts and raisins
            . . . . mashed potato
—but no you.

Now it's New Year and it's Auld Lang Syne
And it's 12 o'clock and I'm feeling fine
Should Auld Acquaintance be Forgot?
I don't know girl, but it hurts a lot
there was
        whisky
         vodka
          dry Martini (stirred
            but not shaken)
 . . . . and 12 New Year resolutions
—all of them about you.

So it's all the best for the year ahead
As I stagger upstairs and into bed
Then I looked at the pillow by my side
. . . . I tell you baby I almost cried
there'll be
                    Autumn
                    Summer
                        Spring
                            . . . . and Winter
—all of them without you.

ADRIAN HENRI

Unknown Shores

AFTER THÉOPHILE GAUTIER

Okay, my starsick beauty!—
blue jeans and tilting breasts,
child of Canaverel—
where would you like to go?

Shall we set course for Mars,
or Venus's green sea,
Aldebaran the golden,
or Tycho Brahe's Nova,
the moons of Sagitta,
or Vega's colonies?

School-minching, bronze Diane,
bane of the launching-pads—
I may not ask again:
wherever you would go

my rocket-head can turn
at will to your command—
to pluck the flowers of snow
that grow on Pluto, or
Capella-wards, to pluck
the roots of asphodel?

I may not ask again:
where would you like to go?

Have you a star, she says,
O any faithful sun
where love does not eclipse?
. . . (The countdown slurs and slips).
—Ah child, if that star shines,
it is in chartless skies,

I do not know of such!
But come, where will you go?

D. M. THOMAS

The Educators

In their
limousines the
teachers come: by
hundreds. O the
square is
blackened with dark suits, with grave
scholastic faces. They
wait to be summoned.
                         These are the
educators, the
father-figures. O you could
warm with love for the firm lips, the
responsible foreheads. Their
ties are strongly set, between their collars. They
pass with dignity the exasperation of waiting.

A
bell rings. They turn. On the
wide steps my
dwarf is standing, both hands raised. He
cackles with laughter. Welcome, he cries, welcome
to our elaborate Palace. It is indeed. He
is tumbling in cartwheels over the steps. The
teachers turn to each other their grave faces.

With
a single grab they have him up by the shoulders. They
dismantle him. Limbs, O
limbs and delicate organs, limbs and
guts, eyes, the tongue, the
lobes of the brain, glands; tonsils, several

eyes, limbs, the tongue,
a kidney, pants, livers, more
kidneys, limbs, the tongue
pass from hand to hand, in their serious hands. He is
utterly gone. Wide
crumbling steps.

They
return to their cars. They
drive off smoothly, without disorder;
watching the road.

D. M. BLACK

Evolution

One wave
sucking the shingle
and three birds
in a white sky

one man
and one idea
two workmen
and a concrete mixer

one wave
shingle
white walls
bird and sky

two workmen
and a concrete mixer

white walls
wave and windows
bird and sky

wave and white rooms
walls and windows
lights and sky

five hundred men
and a computer

desks and days
white walls
lights and
one computer

rooms and men
lights
one computer
desks and days

rooms and windows
desks and lights
lights and days
and days and rooms
desks and rooms
days and lights
daylight in
dayrooms
and days
in desks
and days
in days

and one man
mad
dreaming of

one wave
sucking the shingle
and three birds
in a wide sky

EDWIN BROCK

French Persian Cats
having a Ball

chat
shah shah
    chat
       chat shah cha ha
       shah chat cha ha
    shah
    chat
  cha
  cha

           ha
          chat
          chat
        chatshahchat
     chachacha   chachacha
       shahchatshah
         shah
         shah
          ha

cha
cha
chatcha
  cha
shahcha
  cha
  chatcha
    cha
  shahcha
    cha
    cha

       sh   ch
        aha
       ch   sh

EDWIN MORGAN

214

The Computer's First Christmas Card

```
jollymerry
hollyberry
jollyberry
merryholly
happyjolly
jollyjelly
jellybelly
bellymerry
hollyheppy
jollyMolly
marryJerry
merryHarry
hoppyBarry
heppyJarry
boppyheppy
berryjorry
jorryjolly
moppyjelly
Mollymerry
Jerryjolly
bellyboppy
jorryhoppy
hollymoppy
Barrymerry
Jarryhappy
happyboppy
boppyjolly
jollymerry
merrymerry
merrymerry
merryChris
ammerryasa
Chrismerry
asMERRYCHR
YSANTHEMUM
```

EDWIN MORGAN

Index of Authors

Index of First Lines

217

Index of Titles

222